THE M

The Power of Positive Self-Talk in the Mind Game of Golf

Gratitude Golf Publishing
Columbus, Ohio

Books may be purchased in quantity and/or special sales available to corporations, professional associations, and other organizations, by contacting publisher, Gratitude Golf Publishing, at 614-208-5719, or by email at alecia@gratitudegolf.com.

Published by: Gratitude Golf Publishing, Columbus, Ohio
Cover Design by: Lisa M. Marek, Graphic Designer
Fat Cat Art Studio, St. Paul, MN
www.fatcatartstudio.com

First Printing, 2016

ISBN-13: 978-1532825415
ISBN-10: 1532825412
First Edition
Printed in the United States of America

To contact Gratitude Golf, LLC, please visit the website at:
www.gratitudegolf.com

TABLE OF CONTENTS

DEDICATION

I dedicate this book, first and foremost, to all my students, who over the last 30 years, have helped me become the instructor I am today and taught ME so many lessons! To all of you, my gratitude is deep and you will have an indelible place in my heart for the rest of my life. To Dan Keiser and family, what more can I say except... "Life before the Keiser's and life after the Keiser's," I cannot express to you how much your love and support has meant to me and how special you all are. To my three beautiful children, Jay, Erin, and Nathan, who have taught me to continue striving to be the best version of a mother I can be, I love you so much and am so blessed to have you in my life.

To one of my dearest friends and step-daughter, Kirsten, who I can count on for anything and such a supporter of my ideas, you have always believed in me...thank you. And of course, to my beloved husband and soulmate, Dean, who has listened to my dreams and ideas for so long, loved and supported me through it all, and never gave up on me, I love you. Lastly, to my sweet, dear mother Lila, who brought me into this world, has always been my biggest fan, loves me with the purest of unconditional love, and most importantly, was the one who always told me I should write a book! Well, Mom, with abounding love, I can say... "This one's for you."

A special thanks to Dr. Shad Helmstetter who has been there for me during this entire process with encouragement and insight. Your friendship and guidance has been invaluable and I am so grateful for your support. YOU are incredible!

INTRODUCTION

This book is written for golfers of all levels, but just as importantly, it's written for non-golfers. Yes, I am a long-time golf professional, and yes, that's what motivated me to write this book, but the message I intend to deliver goes far beyond the lesson tee and reaches into the heart of humanity and life itself.

For many years, I have felt strongly that golf was the vehicle for me to send a "life message" when the opportunity arose. In most cases, and often just by chance, I would discover a life lesson during the golf lesson. Generally, it would be one that stirred the emotional spirit and soul of the golfer standing before me, and raised their awareness of what was the *real* issue.

I knew there was something profound about my intent to help others, but not until I discovered self-talk did I realize how incredibly important the message was. And when I began to understand that I could combine self-talk and golf to help my students, it made my purpose even more passionate.

For this book, I have taken words from golf and life that can have a double meaning. I assigned them chapter titles, and intertwined the importance of what we say to ourselves about each of them, to help my students realize how much they are either enhancing or self-sabotaging their goals and potential in these areas. The difference will be, whether one is operating from a positive or negative frame of mind, as both have a powerful influence on the outcome.

For almost my entire career, I have used the formula below to try to bring to the attention of my students the fact that a golf score involves many factors. The formula is simple, yet profound, and it goes like this:

POTENTIAL – INTERFERENCE = PERFORMANCE

I was introduced to this many years ago at an LPGA event, and I have used it as a reference ever since, to make a point that when there is interference in your life, it will affect your performance. We were all born with unlimited potential. Add a certain amount of interference and you will get a diminished outcome. More interference, a less desirable outcome, less interference, a more desirable outcome. It's that simple!

So, let's take a look at what might be examples of interference. How about from the golfing perspective first? There's always a chance you may have to play with someone with whom you don't have a good chemistry or, in less subtle terms...you don't really like them.

I have heard examples of this such as: my not-so-favorite in-laws, an arch rival, an obnoxiously loud person who talks too much, or even someone who is a pretty good golfer, but complains or whines all the way around the course about their performance (even when they happen to be playing better than others in the foursome.) Their negative attitude brought other people down.

What kind of self-talk might you find yourself saying when trying to deal with other people who are causing major distractions during a round of golf? Is it the self-talk that sustains you in your belief that they cause your stress, thus, you will play badly? Do you find yourself blaming your poor play on something or someone other than yourself and making excuses, so you don't "look bad?"

Self-talk that is positive, can shield you from all this chaos and keep you in a comfortable, peaceful state of mind knowing that ultimately, it is only you against the golf course.

Now let's look at the advantages of positive self-talk from a life perspective. In this, the 21ˢᵗ century, the world is fast-paced and we all try to keep up with it. If we don't have the awareness or tools to help us slow down and keep things in perspective, we can get caught up in a race against time, ourselves, and the world around us. It begins to feel like life is out of balance.

Once you leave your driveway and hit the road to your destination, it's possible that you may encounter a road rage driver, or it could be someone you are close to may have hurt your feelings or said something unkind to you; or a loved one is ill or passed away. Any or all of these and many others, will leave you feeling emotional.

On an even more personal level, you yourself might be dealing with health issues, your self-esteem could be low, you may be fighting depression, there is divorce in the family, you have school pressures, you dislike your job and/or have an overload of responsibilities...and the list can go on and on.

All of these factors, whether pertaining to golf or other aspects of life, can play a huge role in your outcome at the end of each day. If self-talk during these difficult times sends continuous, endless messages that are negative or filled with frustration and anger, then over time they become superhighways in the brain, and negative belief systems that are most certain to become your reality, will take a toll on your life.

Once those belief systems become "real-ized", the next thing you know, your reality has put limitations on your potential. It's a slippery slope. The single most important factor for people to recognize and become mindful of, whether in their daily lives or on the golf course, is the power of *what they say when they talk to themselves*. This applies to both our positive and negative thoughts.

Our self-talk directs us to where we send our thoughts most often, and to which superhighways we are creating. When times are challenging, we need to be in control of our thoughts and send as much positivity to our brain as possible.

The 'Missing Link', as I refer to it now, and the title of this book, is the idea regarding self-talk that Dr. Shad Helmstetter has studied and researched for over 40 years. He has found that scientifically, medically and neurologically, our brains are changing until the moment we die. This is called *neuroplasticity*. During our entire lifetime, we have the ability to re-wire our brain, actually changing its physical structure, and counteract all the interference we find ourselves experiencing every day through our personal self-talk.

What is Self-Talk?

Self-talk is everything we say to ourselves, whether in our thoughts or out loud, about ourselves and our lives. It works together with the moments we experience, things we hear from others, read, and observe, regarding ourselves, our world, and our lives, to form the beliefs we hold about ourselves and our potential.

What is Neuroplasticity? *Neuroplasticity is the ability of the brain to physically change according to the programming it gets from us, creating new pathways of neurons and receptors in such a way that our most repeated input creates the strongest pathways and the most powerful programs for the management of our lives.*

*It's the repetition of affirmations that lead to belief.
And once that belief becomes a deep conviction,
things begin to happen."
--Mohammed Ali*

Dr. Helmstetter states that researchers have found that 77% or more of what we say to ourselves, what we hear, read, and see in the midst of our daily lives, is harmful or works against us! That, my friends, is a very large percentage! And without some sort of help to thwart off the negativity, we are in for a pretty rough and rocky road.

More importantly, it is very probable that we will not reach our full potential or even come close to it, if we do nothing about it and continue to live life on auto-pilot.

Back in 2011, while I was in network marketing, I was introduced to self-talk by reading a book by Dr. Helmstetter, titled **"What To Say When You Talk To Your Self."** I must admit that, from that moment on, my life has literally changed on all levels, in both my personal and professional world.

The most impactful moment was when I read the section in the book that said we will take our first breath and our last breath by ourselves and, in reality, we have the right to create whatever story we want in between. It's our story to write! Why would we ever let anyone else write that script? And why would we ever choose negativity over embracing a positive outlook on life? As I read, a light bulb came on for me, and I soon began to realize what had happened to me in my life and in my golfing career as a competitive player. My self-talk had dictated my path and outcomes.

Then one day, as I was listening to the stories of my students, I began to realize that they were doing the same exact thing. Every single one of them, from beginner to advanced players...and I mean EVERY SINGLE ONE! Their own belief systems from their experiences and self-talk, were creating a self-sabotaging environment and results.

They had so many roadblocks set up in their mind about what they could *not* do, and this put limitations on their goals. Once I unraveled the unnecessary beliefs or patterns, they started to realize that they, themselves, were part of the problem! They were holding themselves back. Through our conversations, they became mindful of the situation. They began to give themselves permission to search for a better, more productive way to success, and choose a positive path instead.

With more mindfulness and being able to make an intentional choice for change, you can begin to take the first step. It is an enlightening concept to embrace and one I sincerely hope you will set into motion in your life.

It's when one begins truly to understand the concept of self-talk, and understand that the "strongest program always wins", that change for the better will begin to commence. So for you, the first step will be the introduction to self-talk in general, and knowing what *really* is happening.

Whatever you have been rehearsing in your mind, through all your years until now, is what is going to prevail. In other words, if you have had years of past negative self-talk on the golf course and during practice sessions, it will be your default program under stress, until you start to reprogram your thoughts by repeating positive self-talk.

It's a fact…we were all born with unlimited potential and promise. Somewhere along the way, we started to hear and believe specific statements about ourselves, rehearsed them, and to believe them be true. They have since become our reality.

What thoughts do you have about yourself and the world around you, that may be stopping you from reaching your full potential? What limitations are you subconsciously putting on yourself? How frustrated have you become? Let's take a look at the parallels of golf and life, and how our self-talk can affect our outcomes, either positively or negatively.

It's up to you to make the choice and have the desire to change. I had heard this below statement often in my life, before it actually made its mark on me, but when you are ready to pay attention to it, it is incredible what it can do for you. *"If you want something to change…you must change."* Today, you can make a conscious decision to start on a new path to a better future, filled with hope and promise, by understanding the importance of the "Missing Link!" It's time to make a choice…a positive one. Enjoy the ride…

The Missing Link

Foreword by Shad Helmstetter, Ph.D.

There is a secret, actually many of them, lying in wait in *The Missing Link*. During the time of more than thirty years of writing in the field of personal growth, and studying the subject of why some people manage to create exceptional lives for themselves, while others do not, I had found the game of golf, and the mastery of the game, to be an almost perfect metaphor for the game of life. But I had never found that metaphor put into words— and so well identified—until Alecia Larsen, a master of both golf and life, brought it to life in this book.

We can thank Alecia's long experience in teaching golf and its many complex facets to her students for creating the fertile ground from which this book sprang. But it was her keen insight and observation of the attitudes, emotions, and mental demands that the game of golf created in those students that showed there was a clear and missing link between the physical requirements of the game and the mental requirements of the player. It was a subject that was occasionally discussed or written about, but never before had anyone shown the direct relationship between something as important as their own internal self-talk and the results of their game. What Alecia found was that the link and the results were profound.

When the field of neuroscience proved that thoughts themselves, especially the powerful messages of self-talk, literally wire and rewire neural networks into the brain, and that the brain then acts on those messages as though they were true, the link between positive self-talk and performance became scientifically clear. This has never been truer than in the game of golf; your self-talk and your game will always go hand-in-hand. But it was when Alecia Larsen showed us that the game itself was a metaphor for the life we live outside of the game, that her insight gave us a new awareness of both golf and living.

What Alecia found was that the two are inseparable—the attitudes and skills you hone for a winning game are identical to the attitudes and skills that make a more successful life.

The kind of self-talk that rewires your brain for excelling in the game of golf is identical to the kind of positive self-talk we have learned to use to rewire our brains for winning at life.

As a trained professional in the world of golf, Alecia understands the needs and requirements of both the golfer and the game. As a Certified Self-Talk Trainer™ working with attitude and positive mental programming, she understands how the brain works, and how to wire it for maximum effectiveness. The result of this unique combination of skills is the book you now hold or are listening to. It defines beautifully and clearly each important step, mentally and physically, that leads to high performance.

In introducing this book I would be remiss not to express a third quality that Alecia Larsen brings to the work, and that is the quality of 'heart.' She has a big one. Someone without the deep sense of empathy that Alecia has for her students may have failed to discover the secret, or see so clearly the missing link between self-talk—rewiring the brain for success—and personal excellence in the game of golf. She has a quality of caring, and an openness and clarity that is both refreshing and instructive, that you'll find throughout this exceptional book.

This book will definitely help you improve your game, and along with it, your life.

Shad Helmstetter, Ph.D.

Chapter 1

WE ALL START SOMEWHERE

"A journey of a thousand miles,
must begin with a single step."
-Lao Tsu

Back in 1966 when I was five years old, my mother put me on a bus, in the hands of a very trusted family friend, to go on my very first swim meet as a competitive swimmer. This is my earliest memory of a personal sporting event, and to my knowledge, I had absolutely no fear!

I was in the company of trusted adults, my fellow teammates/friends and chaperones, and I was off into the big world, with one goal in mind...to win a race. I don't actually remember the outcome of the swim meet races, but I do know that my mindset was such that I was out to prove something to myself.

I knew that when I hit the water, all I was going to do was swim as fast as I could to touch the finish line first! Quite certainly the preparation I had put in up to that point at practices, was going to help me during the weekend. I was ready, confident and primed to give it my all. I felt really good about it.

From that moment forward, competitiveness was in my blood. I was on a direct path to wanting to win with any endeavor I chose. The list of sports I played is lengthy, including swimming, basketball, racquetball, tennis, track, softball, volleyball, and of course, golf.

My athleticism, that I believe is a gift from God, allowed me to have a short learning curve to whatever sport I decided to take up and I was told many times growing up that I was a "natural athlete."

Competitiveness, however, was the common thread, no matter what I was doing, whether in sports, a card game, marble games on the playground at my elementary school, or trying to catch the biggest fish out of anyone on the boat, I wanted to excel! I always wanted to win and become a master at what I was attempting to learn. Improving upon my skills with whatever I was participating in, was a must.

I continued to swim competitively until I was about the age of 16. By then, basketball had become a huge part of my life. I must admit, it was the first love of my life in the sports world, and I literally, could not get enough of the sport. I played it as much as I possibly could.

*"The way to get started is to
quit talking and begin doing."
--Walt Disney*

Every day in high school, before I had my driver's license, my father would pick me up at lunch hour, around 11:55 am, we were home by 12:00 noon, and I was done eating by 12:10pm. Without delay, I would then head out to the backyard cement driveway to shoot my basketball, as there was never enough time in the day to practice my shooting techniques.

I was obsessed with being the best there was at it, and practiced every second I had a chance! I was shooting from three-point land before the 3-point shot ever existed. It was awesome to launch the basketball from so far out there. I was told the radio announcers would chant during the broadcast, that I was "shooting from the locker rooms!" Being successful was all I thought about. I was passionate about the game, loved what I was doing and very confident.

I played basketball at recess in elementary school, in city recreation programs, competed in the Knights of Columbus free-throw contests, (won on a local, regional and national level), and attended basketball camps whenever I could. In junior high, I yearned to be on the bench with the high school's varsity girls' basketball team. I just wanted to be in the environment, so much so, that when I was an 8th grader I asked the head coach if I could be the "water girl" for the team. I figured the worst he could say to me was no, but he might say yes, and indeed he did!

From there, I went right into a high school basketball career as a freshman, making the varsity as the 6th player coming in, and a starter the next three years.

Throughout my junior high, high school, and college years, I was also an All-Star softball player, played on the high school tennis team, competed in track to stay in shape for basketball, and played basketball and volleyball in college. I also played a lot of racquetball, it was more of a recreational sport for me though, but a lot of fun. To this day, I still play it at my local fitness center, along with shooting some baskets and swimming.

For the next four years, I was fortunate to be a part of a highly successful tenure with the Williston Coyote girls' basketball team, which included 57 straight wins, and three consecutive North Dakota High School state tournament victories. Personally, I was humbled and

14

honored by being chosen as a North Dakota All-State basketball player three times.

Looking back, my teammates and I were fortunate enough to be a part of history, as our girls' basketball program was one of the best in the nation in the mid-to-late 70's. I also played on two very successful college basketball teams. What a thrill to play with so many talented players!

To this day, my former teammates and I are proud of the fact that we were pace setters for female athletics as it stands in the 21st century. It is inspiring to watch many opportunities happen for young girls in many different types of athletics these days!

You might be starting to wonder where golf was for me in this story. Sharing my athletic background was intentional, and sets the stage as a segue into how I became interested in the game. It was divided into two separate phases, with my parents at the helm of the introduction.

This first introduction was watching it somewhat from a distance, at our lake cabin at Blacktail Dam. My father purchased a small, simple cabin about 30 minutes north of my hometown of Williston, North Dakota. It was perfect for our family, and it provided us with some of the fondest memories of my entire lifetime while growing up, until my father passed away in 1995. I will always have deep gratitude for the decision he made to buy that cabin. They were truly the best years of my life.

It was at this cabin and only about 50 yards from the back of our lot, that sat one of the tee boxes to a small, rugged sand greens golf course...right at my fingertips! In fact, the biffy (a word used in the Upper Midwest to describe outdoor toilets, usually an outhouse,) was right next to the fairway. On occasion, it would get hit by an errant drive off the tee box, quite a startling sound when one is inside quietly going about their business!!

On a typical weekend at the lake, we would fill our days with all sorts of fun activities. These would include swimming, waterskiing, fishing, riding in our pontoon, learning how to drive the family car on the gravel roads, sitting by the bonfire in the summer evenings, visiting our neighbor friends at different cabins around the lake, catching fire flies, playing board games on rainy days and, of course, every now and again, going out to play some golf.

Sometimes we'd gather some old golf balls and challenge each other to a contest. Our objective...to see who could try and hit the balls onto the other side of the channel into our neighbors' lot, about 100-125 yards total. I recall when we first started, I was not able to reach the other side of the lake, but the more I played, the more I improved, and in due time, my shots were making land fall. I even had a few encounters where I was pretty apprehensive about taking out some windows in the cabin we were hitting towards, which happened to be my godparents' cabin. Yikes!

My very first memories of golfing however, were not always positive, mainly because I wasn't very good. I topped the ball a lot and was directionally challenged a vast majority of the time. I knew little about the game, but I was well aware of the fact that hitting the ball and hitting it straight, were two of the key elements.

In describing my first golfing experiences to others, I remember telling people "Yes, I've played golf for many years, and my first rounds of golf were with my Dad and brothers. It went something like this...they would hit the ball and drag Alecia, hit the ball and drag Alecia, and would keep doing that over and over, until we were done!"

I was always trying to keep up with them, but because I couldn't hit the ball as far, I was continually falling behind. Not every time I went to play golf, did I enjoy myself. It certainly challenged their patience with me, and for the most part, it seemed I was quite the bother to them, but I still desperately wanted to be a part of the foursome.

Each time we went out to play, we passed by a small pavilion that had the score cards and pencils, and it is then we'd pick one up for our round to keep score, and make a legitimate game out of it. A little green card with a golf pencil to make the round "official" and we were off.

Back in 2009, I had my 30th class reunion and, of course, I had to go out to Blacktail to see how things looked. I strolled around the golf course and wouldn't you know it, I found, on the old worn out pavilion post, in a small box, a scorecard from the very first course I learned the game on. I remember like it was yesterday, standing there with my father, writing our names down on the card, so we could keep our score! The humorous part of this was, on the card, it's claim to fame was it's "The best course by a Dam site!" My dad and I would always have a chuckle or two about that one liner, but we completely agreed, as we loved our little sand green course!

I am certain I could feel his presence with me standing there, as my eyes swelled up with tears, and I embraced the moment...his spirit was close by. What a treasured memory for me! This is where it all began for me as the original introduction of golf from the prairies of North Dakota!

My appreciation for learning on a course with sand greens is very sentimental to me. These types of courses are a very rare find these days, and as I write this, I often wonder how many of you have ever played on sand greens. If you get a chance, I would encourage you to experience one of the ways golf originally began.

With my curiosity, I did some research on sand green golf courses and found an interesting article from Golf Digest on featured stories of golf courses and travel in July of 2013. It gives a brief description of the culture of sand green golf courses and states, "Sand-green courses, of which there are an estimated 100 or so left in the United States, mostly nine-holers in the Great Plains, offer about as basic a golf experience as a person can have. Fairways are usually mowed once a week, and the grass is as green as Mother Nature -- not a superintendent or club president -- decides it should be. Situated in small towns and rural locales, sand-green courses are about camaraderie and competition not finely manicured turf or fancy clubhouses. (There may be an important lesson in that attitude.)"

So there is the story about where, when, and how I started the first phase of my life with golf. When I began to better understand the depth of the game of golf, in my spare time at the lake, I became personally challenged to improve, and would go out on my own and practice. The only experience I had with any kind of instruction on how to get better, was having my dad tell me a few things and by watching others.

When I think about my father helping me, I have to chuckle though. I'm surprised I can play as well as I can, considering the fact that he originally taught me how to play and he played golf with a cross handed grip...not in putting, but with his full swing! He's the only person I know who had a hole in one with such an incredibly unorthodox grip, but he could hit it straight!

He and his best friend, Larrie, always played golf together and I loved to watch how much fun they had. That's the true gift of the game, being together with people we love to spend time with. I thank him for being one of the most influential people introducing me to this amazing sport.

In my early years, I also have very fond memories of visiting my great uncle's farm in Minot, ND. My Uncle Mort would ask me to come on out to the edge of his wheat fields and he would watch me hit golf balls far out into the tall tassels of the field, where they would propel off my club face, take shape like a rainbow, and disappear into the wheat without a sound.

He was always a big fan of my golf swing, as he himself was a golfer, and his praise and positive feedback was probably what kept me believing that someday I really could be good, myself. Many years later, I won one of my two North Dakota State Amateur titles in Minot, and I know he would have been so proud!

Up until his last days on the farm, while in his wheelchair before he died of cancer, he continued to ask me to swing by the wheat fields. These times will always be some of my most sentimental memories I carry in my heart. Again, one of those situations where golf provides us with so many of those cherished life moments and opportunities, to connect us with friends and family members, and genuinely gives it the honorable title of the "game of a lifetime!"

After my high school days were over, I remember one day a college teammate of mine and I were talking about getting a summer job, and we thought it would be fun to work outside. With that, we decided to apply at the local 9-hole private golf course in town, the Williston Country Club.

Much to our surprise we got the job and we began working on the grounds crew. Watering the course, whipping the greens, (something not done anymore with the latest, modernized equipment) mowing the fairways, roughs, and greens, working in the bunkers, cutting cups, pretty much any job that was required to prepare the golf course for play, was our job description.

It was at this club that I met my first husband, John, and I would be remiss if I didn't mention that he was also very instrumental in getting me obsessed with golf. He allowed me frequent opportunities to travel the country, attend many a golf school, play beautiful golf courses, create a plethora of cherished memories, and receive golf instruction from some of the best instructors in the world.

So for that, I am deeply grateful for the gift he gave me, to enhance my golfing career. Together, at this little 9-hole course, we played a great deal of golf together and we eventually introduced golf to our three children at this club.

In the second phase of my career, it was my mother who played an integral part in my introduction to the game and taking it to the next level.

> *"The secret to getting ahead*
> *is getting started."*
> *--Mark Twain*

In about the year 1980, she encouraged me to take a golf lesson with the local pro (at the 9-hole golf course I worked at), who moved to

North Dakota from California after he married our family's babysitter from many years prior. Often, my mom would ask me, "Why don't you just take one lesson with Mike, and just see how it goes."

After weeks and maybe even months of her continuing to repeat this request, I wanted to get her to stop asking me about it, so I decided I would take ONE golf lesson, in hopes that she would be satisfied and stop asking! So it was here, where the story of my "real" golfing career started.

Our driving range, where one typically would look to hone their skills, was less than desirable, and I used to call it a cow pasture! I would search for lone patches of grass from which to be able to hit balls, and without fail, these areas of grass were surrounded by huge white patches of alkali, which comprised most of the soil there. There were so few range balls at the club, that when I wanted to practice, I would have to pick up all the range balls after I hit them, and return to the golf shop when I was finished.

The range was strategically placed (I say that with a bit of sarcasm) about 100 yards just to the right of number one tee box, so you were pretty much in the firing line of people coming off the first tee! This problem was supposedly solved by putting in 8 to 10 big telephone poles with netting draped on them, so you were protected from those errant tee shots from golfers on #1 tee box, while you were on the range hitting balls and practicing. I guess that was supposed to give you peace of mind. It was there where I took my very first lesson.

It was a nice warm, summer day when I approached Mike to book a lesson with him, and I remember it like it was yesterday. Our lesson was around 1:00 in the afternoon. Mike got a small bucket of 25-30 range balls and asked me to bring my seven iron only. He stood there and watched me hit ball after ball until they were all gone, and then proceeded to say one thing to me: "That was great, and the only comment I will make to you is.... you can be as good as you want to be!" With that, he smiled at me and walked back into the clubhouse!

After he left me, I was intrigued by the comment that he had made, even though I didn't quite know what to do with it. For the next few minutes, I found myself sitting there dreaming about what that could possibly mean to me and my future with golf.

"A year from now, you may
wish you started today."
--Karen Lamb

19

The reality was that I was living in a very small rural town in northwest North Dakota, with a population of about 10,000 people, and I wasn't quite sure if there was any way out of there to fulfill any kind of dream I had had in my life up to that point, golf-related or otherwise. After all, I was already married and had children and my family was certainly my priority. My dreams were just that...dreams.

Because of fear and responsibility as a mother, my mind immediately put limitations on my dreams. With a bit more thought, however, I picked up some more golf balls and proceeded to hit another bucket, because my competitive nature told me I had to go to work and practice...and I suddenly became determined to improve. My goals were in sight and my dreams were out there to be reached! The road ahead would be filled with ups and downs, but one thing I knew...I wanted to be good!

I've lived and learned a lot between that moment and now, as I write on these pages. I have a compelling message to share and this book is how I have chosen to do it.

I am so blessed to have crossed paths with my mentor and dear friend, Dr. Shad Helmstetter. He has encouraged and supported me in this wonderful journey of writing this book. The purpose? To convey my simple, yet largely-overlooked message to golfers around the world...the fact that golf is so much more than your physical swing. With this awareness, and the knowledge of what else you need, you soon will be on the path to enjoying the game at a much higher level. I have written **The Missing Link** just for *you!*

I know when people seek instruction and practice their game, they are predominantly thinking about the physical elements of the game, and not the mental aspect of it. Their practice is disproportionate to the percentages of their score, and it shows.

Golfers seem to be aware of the fact that there is much to learn about golf, but typically, it narrows down to two major areas: the physical part, which is called the mechanics of the swing, and the mental game. You will even hear people say, "Golf is 90% mental." Yet, little attention is given to actually learning and practicing the mental side to the game. One of the greatest female golfers of all time, Annika Sorenstam, wrote an article on her Facebook page relative to this, and it succinctly makes my point. Annika states:

I'm sure you've heard the expression "The longest distance in golf is between your ears. It may sound funny, but it's really true. Our mind plays games with us on the course, so controlling our thoughts and developing a positive mental approach are crucial to good golf. For example, how many of us hit it great on the range and then we walk to the first tee and something changes? How many of us have had doubt creep in while we're standing over an important putt? Maybe you're someone who gets easily upset and a bad shot or three-putt wrecks your scorecard.

There are many reasons why players need to have a strong mind, even those with the best swings, smoothest putting strokes or greatest feel around the greens. Players with a strong mind perform better because when the time comes to execute a shot, they believe in themselves and emphasize the process, rather than the results. How does one do this? The first thing I learned to do was focus. Focus on yourself. No one knows your game, your strengths or your weaknesses better than you do. Becoming self-aware trains our mind to concentrate on the achievable. This approach allows you to cultivate positive thinking and find your "zone" more often. So, focus on the right things, and you'll find your potential.

Next, avoid using excuses like "My playing partner was so slow," "The pin positions were too tough," "I am tired and my caddie confused me." etc. This type of negative thinking and blame is not productive, it wastes energy and causes you to lose sight of what's important—focusing on yourself and what you can control.

It's fair to say that golfers know the importance of mental training and many renowned golfers say the game is 90% mental. So why do most players continue to spend less than 1% on this aspect of the game? That's your first mental mistake…

I do recommend everyone research and become well-versed in all there is to learn about golf, because there is indeed, a lot to learn about it. But learning early on, that the mental side to golf is so critical to your enjoyment, will only enhance your overall experience. I often tell students that golf is an acquired skill and it does take time to learn, or to improve on your existing game, so be patient with the process, but know the facts.

All of the elements of the game you can learn over time and achieve the skill...one step at a time. It's the *other* element of the game, the 'missing link', that I want to highlight in this book, more than the physical elements.

"How will I make today a great day?
I will start with my attitude, and make it upbeat and positive. I
will review my goals so I know what to do.
I will add to my list, a way to make someone else's
life better. And, I will take my every
breath as though it were my last."
--Dr. Shad Helmstetter

Many golfers have a big void in their instruction, and an imbalance, when it comes to mental preparation. This applies to their own approach, and also, from many instructors teaching to the masses, who may not place enough emphasis on this area.

I truly believe, after 28+ years of teaching, and playing this game both competitively and leisurely for nearly 45 years, that this is the number one issue preventing golfers from improving, enjoying the game more, and reaching their full potential.

Most of the time, golfers are not even mindful of their own self-sabotage making them unwittingly, their own worst enemy! The real problem is that they continue to focus on the physical elements, and discount how important it is to be mentally positive and acquire mental toughness. They keep on seeking golf instruction and changing their swings, thinking that is the problem, while all along neglecting the mental side to golf, and not changing their mindset and old patterns.

The "secret sauce" to improving and having fun with this game is what this book is all about. I invite you to sit back, relax, and enjoy discovering what the majority of golfers overlook when it comes to improving their golf game, or if they are just learning, what causes them so much frustration that they end up quitting and saying that golf wasn't for them or "lessons didn't help."

Let's discover and eliminate any obstacles you might have in your way, and find out how you may be self-sabotaging your potential, so that you can, at last, enjoy this great game that has so many lessons within it to teach us about our golf game, ourselves, and our life!

Chapter 2

FOUNDATION

"Each day my own self-talk wires my brain with a picture
of the person I will become tomorrow. If I am 'down' on me, my
brain will believe it, wire it in, and pull me down. If I am 'up' on
me, my brain will be wired to help me succeed. The truth is, my
tomorrow is up to me."
--Dr. Shad Helmstetter

Foundation is defined in the dictionary as "The basis or groundwork for anything."

When I ponder the word foundation, there are more "big picture" thoughts that come to mind pertaining to life in general. However, we know the parallels between golf and life are strong, and I find myself contemplating what it means for golf as well, and the impact it has on my students.

Relating "foundation" to life, I think about where were you born and raised, what kind of environment surrounded you. Was it healthy, supportive, life-giving, or was it unhealthy, non-supportive, and energy draining? Positive or negative reinforcement?

In golf, when and how were you introduced to the game--at an early age or later in life? Did you have access to a golf course or were you nowhere near one? Did you get instruction or were you self-taught? Did you learn in comfortable/safe conditions or was it filled with stress?

All of us were born and placed into an environment we didn't necessarily choose, and were exposed to family systems and beliefs that may or may not have been in our favor. Either way, there was a foundation built, and the groundwork was laid for us in our younger years, and we learned a specific culture through our experiences that somewhat molded us into who we are today.

As we grow older we can make our own decisions and mold the platform the way we want our foundation to look. We will make conscious decisions according to our own preferences and values, and to a large extent, this will be how our life is played out.

We can choose a more solid platform and it will withstand the test of time, with long term satisfaction as a goal, or we can choose one that might cut corners and give us immediate gratification. The second of these will create a shoddy foundation and eventually will have shoddy consequences on some level.

Regarding the difference between the two choices, I can't help but think about one of my favorite quotes from Dr. Wayne Dyer when he said, "We are only one thought away from changing our life." Choose wisely.

In a conversation with my husband, a retired Lutheran pastor, I brought up this chapter on foundation. He immediately referenced the following Bible verse:

Matthew 7: 25-27

"And the rain fell, and the floods came, and the winds blew and slammed against that house; and yet it did not fall, for it had been founded on the rock.
"Everyone who hears these words of Mine and does not act on them, will be like a foolish man who built his house on the sand. "The rain fell, and the floods came, and the winds blew and slammed against that house; and it fell-- and great was its fall."

When giving thought to "foundation", the words that come to mind for me are stability, strength, and support. I have always thought of the foundational concept in life, in terms of a cement foundation being built for a house, that is secure and one we can count on.

The foundations that we develop over time, are the ones that we live out in our daily lives, pertaining to the core values in our family systems, in hopes they are going to be strong and positive.

Now, I must mention, I respect everyone's various faith backgrounds, but in this context, I am encouraging you to consider the message in this particular Bible scripture, relative to how you choose to live out your life and set up your foundation. You may have come from a positive or negative environment, but you still have choices. As Dr. Dyer said… "choose wisely."

First, you have a choice to continue on with positive reinforcement to yourself and others. Or another choice is, if you happen to come from a negative environment, you can make a change and start to live life more fully, with an eventual paradigm shift to the positive reinforcement side of the world.

You can start to build your foundation for life more solidly around numerous core values such as integrity, gratitude, compassion, respect, patience, love and understanding, to name a few. Or the last option, and one we hope you don't choose, is to continue to live in a negative world, where frustration, stress, and unhappiness abound, and there always seems to be something "missing" in life.

> *"Good order is the*
> *foundation of all things."*
> *--Edmund Burke*

Each approach will have a ripple effect on your life, either positive or negative, it's really your choice. Each year that I teach, I become more aware of the evidence that some students are performing at less than their full potential. And it's not entirely because of swing mechanics; rather a large part is because of negative self-talk.

There's a 'missing link' to reaching your full potential and that 'missing link' is positive, reinforcing self-talk as the structural foundation. Imagine your first step in building the foundation of your home. The same holds true in your golf game and in your life, it's a critical building block to your future. What does this first important step look like for you?

It's what you say repeatedly to yourself that establishes your belief systems and puts your goals within reach--or sets limitations on you and far from your reach. Whatever you repeat the most, becomes the strongest program. Positive self-talk is the solid foundation in both the mental game of golf and in your daily life. With it you thrive, without it, you likely will not.

With your golf game, you can choose to appreciate and understand the importance of fundamentals, in both the mechanical and mental game, or you can play compensating error golf with poor fundamentals and negative self-talk, with the consequences being largely punitive. Once again, it's your choice.

I often tell my students, "Practice what you want, don't practice what you don't want." If you want positive results, you must practice with positive self-talk. On the physical side, you want solid, fundamental mechanical practice, making desired changes towards steady improvement and new habits.

As a golf instructor, I realize that good golf shots give us confidence, but at the end of the day, it is imperative that you practice from the foundation of positive self-talk. Otherwise, the shots you are seeking will

25

happen less often, and the mechanics you are trying to repeat will not develop.

As a child growing up, I experienced mostly a strong, loving foundation in our home with positive reinforcement from both of my parents. I realize now that, outside of my home life, somewhere along my timeline, I somehow began to develop a fear of failure. I started thinking about failure too much, and I didn't want to let anyone down, in any area of my life, including myself.

My work ethic became stronger, but because of fear and doubt, it diminished my success and eventually became the reality for me. Even though I had a lot of athletic talent, I often got in my own way. I wanted to win and excel all the time, and when I didn't, I thought I was a failure. My self-talk changed and it was programming me negatively.

"Morale and attitude are
fundamentals to success."
--Bud Wilkinson

My foundational thought process had changed and it became a house built on sand. Listening to self-talk would have been my solution, it truly was the 'missing link' for me. This is why I am so adamant about sharing my story with you.

I *know* this can help *you!* I strongly feel that golfers who are just learning the game, or seeking a better game, are experiencing one of three things:

1) Avoiding or not interested in learning more about the mental side to golf.

2) Don't know how important it is to their game and how it affects their learning process.

3) Have no idea where to start finding out more about it and how to start making the change.

I lament that I didn't have the self-talk tool back in those days, and I knew of no one to coach me through those dark, self-sabotaging, negative times in my golfing career. But now my passion has shifted towards making sure you, and all golfers around the world, can start to reach their full potential through positive self-talk, and experience the joy of having their golf game built on a strong, stable foundation! For that reason, I am sharing this all-important message with you. If I were more aware of the long term side effects of the toxicity I was creating for myself, I would never have chosen to continue on that path.

**"No one can make you feel inferior
without your consent."
--Eleanor Roosevelt**

Frequently, I have first-time students coming to the lesson tee and I will ask them to share with me what type of "issues" they are having with their game. They often will tell me what they think their problem is, and it could be mechanical and/or a mental game issue. The next comment they make is, "But, I don't know how to fix it...that's why I am here!"

If you start out with proper fundamentals, a rock solid foundation, you will have a better understanding of the importance of building your swing from the ground up. You will appreciate and realize the importance of how essential the fundamentals are.

Beginner golfers who have this insight into the importance of a solid foundation early on, come to the lesson tee and tell me they want to learn the "right way" so they don't have a chance to learn any bad habits from the start. This approach naturally promotes positive self-talk and certainly relieves the mental anxiety they would experience if they learned improperly and played more from the fear and doubt mode.

No, it's not so easy when you have just made a triple bogey, feeling very angry and someone in the moment, comes up to you and says "Just take a deep breath, it's okay." You're probably feeling like dumping water over their head when they say that, as it is *not* easy to let those emotions go if you haven't practiced *how* to do that. Positive self-talk *is* a foundational tool to help you through those moments.

An appropriate question for me would have been one I ask my students occasionally, "If I talked to you the way you talked to you...would you allow me to be your friend?" The answer always has been, 'No way!' There is no logical reason you should be so hard on yourself, it just simply isn't worth it, and what do you gain from it? Nothing...except program negativity into your brain to generate undesirable outcomes and continue to have feelings of inadequacy.

Encourage yourself, lift yourself up, and be your own best friend. I actually have heard commentators on television broadcasts referring to negative self-talk, saying it is just part of the game! Well, I am here to tell you that you have a choice and *it doesn't have to be part of **your** game!!* Make the choice today to start on a new path to transform your game into an amazing experience.

What I know from experience as an instructor is, through consistent effort, you can practice and work hard enough to get your swing repetitively sound. But...if you have a mental meltdown on the course and let your emotions and negative beliefs control you, there is nothing anyone can do about that, until you begin to re-wire your thoughts and change your beliefs and patterns. And it *will* adversely affect your outcome.

From the mental side of the game, positive self-talk IS the key component and foundation that you, as a golfer, or any athlete for that matter, need after you have physically prepared for action. It truly is then the "missing link."

It perplexes me to see how many golfers find it acceptable to play from such harsh mental conditions and personally attack themselves all the time. Jack Nicklaus called golfers masochistic; he said they love to be hard on themselves.

Why is that? Why is it that you take up a game to have fun and enjoy the outdoors, then you beat yourself up about various things such as a missed putt, bad drive off the tee box, or any other shot you don't feel is acceptable, and then you allow this to become the norm? There's not a whole lot of logic to this behavior, and I am committed to show you how to end this madness in your golf game and in your life. I speak this from personal experience and sharing this message so you may not endure the same. I do know there is one thing you will gain from being hard on yourself, increased frustration. Build your game and your life around a solid foundation built on the rock of positive self-talk, and it will pay dividends!

There are physical fundamentals in every sport, and in golf instruction, I focus on six areas. These would include grip, aim, posture, and ball position, as the originals. I add two more fundamentals in my teaching: mindset and tension level.

All of these play a significant role in the consistency of your game, but the last two fall more under the category of the mental side of golf.

When observing a student's golf swing on the lesson tee, I am steadily aware of their foundation, and I always start there to make sure they are on solid ground, in order to create a consistent golf game overall.

If this is not done, a person can develop a pattern called "two wrongs to make a right" --two compensating errors to acquire a desired outcome, which is a foundation built on sand. This compensating-errors approach does not allow you to experience "good" misses, and these are the types of misses you want, as they aren't as consequential on your scorecard.

> *"Get the fundamentals down and*
> *the level of everything you do will rise."*
> *--Michael Jordan*

I pay so much attention to this because while I was a Lead Instructor for the Golf Digest Schools in 2000-2001, one of the most important concepts I learned was that 90% of the problems you have with your game, are due to something you do incorrectly *before* you start swinging.

A very large percentage, and it deserves our attention. If you are sound in this area, your game will be much more consistent. You should never underestimate its importance. And, by the way, in your off-season, this is a perfect time to sharpen or develop your fundamentals. Master them in the cold months, and you are more ready to take it to the course when the temperatures warm up.

For those lower handicap golfers, keeping your basics sharp is the key to keeping your game consistent. I have heard it over and over again, when I listen to broadcasters and other great teachers talk about their experiences with players on the PGA and LPGA tour. They mention making a very slight change in a fundamental and it puts the player right back on track.

A good example of this was a story about Phil Mickelson. I was watching a PGA tour event on television one Sunday and the winner of the tournament turned out to be Phil. When they interviewed him and asked him what he did differently this week as opposed to last week when he missed the cut, he responded by saying something like: "Well, you might think this is kind of crazy, but I flew my swing coach out here and after watching me swing for a while, he found something about my posture he didn't like, changed it a bit and I felt much more comfortable. It made all the difference in the world."

Yes!! Spot on! One of the best in the world just said that all his coach did was change his posture a bit and he started hitting the ball better. Confirmation of my commitment as an instructor, to continue making this an integral part of my approach to teaching. A secondary benefit of this is, it puts you in a more positive state of mind with confidence, and increases your likelihood of having a positive outcome, which always breeds positive self-talk.

So, we know that in pretty much everything you do, from daily life, to business, sports, and everything in between, a good foundation is what makes you feel more solid, stable and organized. It puts you in a place where you have a greater chance to live life to your full potential.

You were born perfect in God's eyes, with unlimited promise and potential. May you begin to see the beauty in your own spirit and soul, enough to be your own best friend and coach, on a solid foundation built on positive self-talk.

GOLF LESSON FROM CHAPTER 2

Fundamentals are the foundation to build your golf game on; they are what give you the structure to move forward for a consistent game. Bobby Jones once said, "You can't expect to play better unless you learn the fundamentals of the swing." Understand the importance of the mental game foundation as well, practice it as much as your mechanics, and apply it every time you swing a golf club.

LIFE LESSON FROM CHAPTER 2

In life, when we set out to build our foundation, we are faced with the choice to build it on rock or on sand. Let your foundation be a stable base that provides you with the strength you need to get through life. Let your positive self-talk be a small pebble that sends out a BIG ripple effect into your life and into others, so you can live life to the fullest with a solid foundation for success and make a difference. You deserve it, it's yours for the asking, and now you can take the necessary steps to create that better life you have longed for.

PERSONAL REFLECTION AND INSIGHTS FROM CHAPTER 2

_____

_____

_____

_____

_____

_____

_____

_____

_____

_____

_____

_____

_____

_____

_____

_____

_____

Chapter 3

PREPARATION

> *"You can never guarantee you'll be
> the smartest person in the room,
> but there is no excuse for not being
> the most prepared."*
> *--Brendan Paddick*

Before I even get out of bed in the morning, I am already talking to myself and rehearsing what my day is going to be filled with. I am in preparation mode for the day. Most of the time, I talk to myself without realizing it, and then once I am mindful of conversation in my head, I have already chanted a few positive comments to get myself ready and get my day started.

It seems with most everything in life, we human beings are always preparing for something. Getting ready to go out the door in the morning for school or work, getting ready to go out for dinner with family or friends, getting ready to go on a date, or to host an event at your home such as thanksgiving or Christmas gatherings, preparing for wedding, birthday and graduations parties, to name a few.

Some of these preparation times are such as those routines we go through in our everyday lives. In either case, it requires us to consider the details in advance, so hopefully, the event or day turns out as we planned.

As mentioned earlier, an example of intentional preparation would be hosting a Thanksgiving or Christmas dinner/gathering at your home. A practice I have personally started in the past few years, is preparing *several* days in advance, instead of just the day before.

I have found that when I do, there is a much greater chance I may enjoy the day more with my family and friends. It gives me additional time to get things done and the opportunity to plan and prepare more extensively.

In reference to autopilot preparation, this would be our daily habits of getting ready for work or school. We know exactly what time we should get up in the morning, have a set of routine steps to accomplish like making our bed, getting dressed, brushing our teeth, putting the coffee on, eating breakfast, etc. and then approximately what time we need to get into the car to reach our destination on time.

Recently, I experienced a "life preparation" moment when I was watching my granddaughters for the first time since they moved back to Ohio and they were staying overnight. The following day, we were going to a Fourth of July parade.

Now, it's been a long time since I had little ones and I had to remember all the things one must bring as necessities. I did a preliminary preparation in my head, as I talked to myself and went through in my mind what I was to bring in the morning.

My preparation wasn't thorough enough, though, as I still found myself having to drive back to the house, because I had forgotten something that was very necessary for the trip...diapers! It was an interesting reminder of how far removed I was from this era in my life, but also, in this case, I should have been even more diligent about my preparation steps.

An analogy I use on the lesson tee about being prepared for situations is one from the classroom. When I ask my students, what type of shot they are attempting to hit, very often I get a response similar to "I'm not sure, I just hit the ball." I tell them that hitting a golf shot without any type of preparation or a target, is like going to take an exam at school without studying at all.

During my high school years, when I studied for a test well in advance, and had prepared for the day it was administered, I was much more relaxed and calm. I was ready for the teacher to hand me the paper so I could get started! My self-talk was strong!

> *"Excellence without effort is as futile*
> *as progress without preparation."*
> *--William Arthur Ward*

On the flip-side of that, if I hadn't prepared well, and I knew it, I was really nervous and couldn't focus as much as I needed to, in order to receive an acceptable grade. And guess what...my self-talk was not so good. Of course, you're going to be nervous for the exam if you have not done the proper preparation, but if you have studied, then you are likely to score well on the test.

Preparation gives us the gift of peace of mind, and confidence...a much greater chance to succeed, and eliminate any negative self-talk. Your self-talk will affect your outcome. The same goes for preparing for a golf shot, if you prepare properly, you increase your odds of hitting the acceptable golf shot that you are seeking. The fact is, your mind will be filled with one of two things; positive or negative self-talk.

In various sports, every single day, there are athletes all around the world preparing for a special event that they have dreamt about competing in, sometimes all of their lives. It's likely they have been working for months or even years towards a vision or goal they are trying to reach.

One thing for sure, they know the importance of preparing properly and continuing to believe in themselves with positive self-talk, and support from family and friends. If we had the opportunity to ask them if negative self-talk or doubt tried to creep into their mind once in a while, I bet we'd know the answer...yes, it's very likely. But with a strong will and systematic preparation, they were ready for it, and replaced it with determination and positivity.

So, being mindful of this fact, what choice will you make to be prepared? What are some necessary steps you might need to think about in order to increase your odds of a positive outcome? Are you fully prepared so you can enjoy the moment?

"You have to rely on your preparation.
You have got to be really passionate and
try to prepare more than anyone else,
and put yourself in a position to succeed. And, when
the moment comes, you get to enjoy, relax, breath,
and rely on your preparation, so that you can perform
and not be anxious or filled with doubt."
--Steve Nash

Such as it is with golf, if we have prepared properly, we may experience more of a flow in the round and with little interference, I sometimes call this synchronicity. Preparation sets the tone. In the golfing world, preparing for a round of golf could have different meanings though, based on the importance of the round for each individual golfer.

In a casual round of golf, there may be some simple preparation steps that take place before getting on the course, compared to a more serious round of golf in the competitive world. I know that most well established golfers have a pretty specific pre-round warm up routine they execute before they take to the course. This is essential to their rhythms, and well thought out routines to their preparation, which builds confidence. In either case, for beginners or established players and everyone in between, being prepared is paramount.

Weather in Ohio, in the early spring, can be quite unpredictable. In April, some of my junior golfers were playing competitively in a Southern Ohio PGA event and were going to be faced with weather elements that were definitely not in their favor, with about an 90%-100% chance of rain, and somewhat low temperatures. I was going to bring to their attention that they had better be packing their rain gear, umbrellas, extra towels, gloves that were in bags to keep them dry, etc., but I decided not to, just to see if their "preparation mindset" was intact.

In my conversations with them before the round, I was happy to find that all of them had taken the necessary steps to be ready, they were prepared. If one ever makes the mistake and does not have all the bases covered in this situation, it's a one-time lesson, and not likely to happen again.

All golfers that have played long enough know that inherent to golf is the uncontrollable weather elements, and having the proper means to deal with them, is one of the most important steps to avoid interference, mental anguish and higher scores. If not prepared, it can breed negativity and have a direct influence on the playing experience.

A young student of mine, in middle school, who just started working with me came to the lesson tee after competing in her first tournament in the summer months. When I asked her to give me a recap of her competitive round the day before, she said, "It was a pretty rough day" and she didn't do very well. I asked her to describe some of those things that "didn't go well," and one of them ironically, had to do with being prepared before the round.

The story began with her saying the weather was very, very hot; she got sunburned, was thirsty most of the time and didn't have enough fluids, and felt low energy because she didn't have anything to eat in her golf bag.

Obviously, the lesson in this situation was pretty clear. She needed to have sunscreen in her bag, any type of fluids to stay hydrated, and also have some nutritional snacks and food handy, to keep her energy level up. Going out unprepared to play golf, in any extreme condition, is sure to result in negative consequences, which will have a direct effect on your mindset and experience in the round.

The other critical area where I see my students make a huge mistake, is in their preparation before a shot they are attempting to execute. Walking up to any shot, not taking inventory on what it should look like (visualization), where you want it to end up, just getting up there and recklessly taking a swing at it, is not, in any way, being prepared.

"Be prepared, work hard, and hope for a little luck. Recognize that the harder you work and the better prepared you are; the more luck you might experience." --Ed Bradley

There is little chance that the forthcoming shot will produce the results you want, and then guess what happens? Fear, doubt, and negative self-talk arrive for your next shot, and literally sometimes even panic. Now you are on a very slippery slope, in a position to have a series of bad shots, followed by a string of bad holes, that are poised to adversely affect your score, once again.

Whew...that was a scary scenario, and one we all want to avoid! How many of you have actually been down that bumpy road? Likely, all of us have been there, but we *do* have an option that will increase the chances of a better end result...it's called being prepared.

I should also add, there are many optimum preparatory factors one should consider, regarding the physical part of golf as well, as stated in the Golf Science book. A few to mention are, having a regular fitness assessment, aerobic fitness, strength and conditioning, diet and nutrition, mobility/stability/flexibility, podiatry, optometry, and management of injuries. Many of these could apply to physical conditioning and staying healthy in general, and not just pertaining to a golf game.

So let's take a look at what a golfer *should* do before a golf shot, to properly prepare, and in technical terms, it's called a *pre-shot routine.*

This routine is something I feel is an absolute necessity, as it fills your mind with preparatory thoughts, and not negative self-talk of fear and doubt.

First, take in all the necessary data, which includes the velocity of wind, pin placements, hazards, the lie of the ball, etc. and the lie will vary depending on where you are located, i.e. tee box, fairway, rough, with club selection next.

The next step is one I encourage all my students to do when choosing a specific target. I tell them to simply ask themselves the following question... "If I could pick this ball up, go out and place it in a perfect position where I would want it to come to rest, when I have finished executing my shot, where would that place be?" Ball is always point "A" and where you want the ball to end up is always point "B." Once that is decided, you have now created your target line and will be able to choose an intermediate target.

37

Chuck Hogan, who is considered one of the foremost authorities in the golf instruction industry, wrote an article about the pre-shot routine. (Chuck has written and produced several books, videos and audio tape programs and developed award winning packages like Nice Shot! and the Player's Course. Additionally, Chuck serves as a frequent contributor to GOLF, Golf Week, Golf Tips, Golf for Women and Senior Golfer.)

He mentioned succinctly, the importance of the pre-shot routine and what it does for us. Mr. Hogan states, "The purpose of the pre-shot routine is twofold. Number one, it insulates you from the waves of interference that are a normal part of playing golf (noise, adverse conditions, negative thinking, etc.). Number two, a good pre-shot routine leads to a 'go' signal, an internal sense that triggers the start of your swing, making that all important transition from pre-swing to in-swing, smooth and trouble free."

I would also like to add, that visualization is a practice all good golfers use before every shot they take, and what every golfer should try to include in their pre-shot routine, no matter what level you are at. Visualize the shot you want to hit, in preparation for the swing to commence, which we know builds confidence.

"Winning can be defined as the
science of being totally prepared."
--George Allen, Sr.

Next comes the mental commitment to the shot you are about to attempt. This is when you are standing over the ball and ready to start your backswing. If you have **any** doubt in your mind at this point and time, you should immediately step away. I call this getting out of a house on fire! It's a tricky moment, as you need to be keenly listening to, or mindful of, any unnecessary chatter that might be going on in your mind.

WARNING.... these are fleeting moments or thoughts that we sometimes don't even know are happening, but can definitely affect our end result. Once we are aware of them, then we can edit and replace them with positive self-talk and the commitment needed for a positive outcome.

Let me share an appropriate metaphor for these fleeting moments I am referring to, with a bit of whimsy. My father used to love to go to the zoo and watch the monkeys swing on the vines from one tree to the next, chasing each other playfully, but carelessly.

So, while standing over the golf ball for only a few seconds before you strike it, I liken these thoughts in your mind to this scenario, thus I lovingly call it "monkey chatter!" These moments can happen briskly and without too much thought or notice, but they are very real and definitely can affect your outcome. They are swift and elusive, but certainly dominate your thoughts.

I highly recommend that you do not try to "get away" with any doubting self-talk at this time, as there is a strong chance that you would then face negative consequences as your end result. Then comes frustration with ourselves and more mental anguish, and once again, we are on the slippery slope! I know, because I have stubbornly tried this the wrong way too many times and each and every time, my results were not good. Yes, I have learned my lesson!

Lastly, you will start your swing and need to trust the motion 100%. There are many moving parts to a golf swing, but those parts make the whole swing complete. I encourage my students to swing back and swing through, with no interruption of motion, and then hold your finish. This takes a positive mental commitment and discipline to stay in the shot until the end.

You can evaluate the shot after it's over and take in the information objectively, so you know what to work on or practice in the future. Do not emotionalize your shot; it will produce no positive effects for you in the upcoming holes to be played.

If you do the previous steps, in *all* of your golf shots, you will be giving yourself the best possible chance to hit an acceptable shot more often! The more acceptable shots you hit, the more you will stay in a relatively positive frame of mind. If you think you should always hit great shots, well then…get ready for some frustration to set in. Golf is not a game of perfect.

I am amazed to see so how many golfers are unprepared to hit a golf ball, and then have very high expectations for a good outcome. How can one expeditiously address the golf ball, randomly hit without any type of preparation, and expect to see a favorable outcome of any sort? If there is no plan there is likely, no good shot. You might be able to pull a shot off now and again, but it won't lead to consistency in your game.

While watching a golf tournament one Sunday, I heard a quote by one of the announcers saying "Luck favors the prepared!" How very true, so here's my suggestion to you, want more luck?…. *be prepared!*

"To be prepared is half the victory!"
--Miguel De Cervantes

Recently, in a playing lesson, a student told me she absolutely knew she wasn't ready to start her swing. Her preparation was inadequate, but yet, still wanted to proceed, quickly start the backswing, and still try to hit a decent golf shot. Her self-talk *hoped* she could pull it off! That was an intentional thought to proceed being unprepared, and clearly a choice I wouldn't recommend.

Mental anguish then starts to multiply and negative self-talk enters in short order. The key is to heighten your awareness of those fleeting moments (monkey chatter) and thoughts, in order for you to edit them and replace with something more positive and productive. Thinking you can get away with haphazardly approaching the ball with no plan or preparation in place, is perilous to your game.

We know through research and scientific studies, that when a person makes a statement, whether to themselves or to someone else about their golf game, abilities, potential, etc., they are programming the brain, either in a positive or negative way. So please, be careful with what you are about to say to yourself regarding any particular situation, as you stand over a golf ball, or in everyday life, remember...you are creating your superhighway!

With all the nuggets shared in this chapter about preparation, I would like to highlight one more thing. While I am obviously emphasizing the importance of preparation, I am also wanting to remind you, that by taking these steps, we are merely trying to increase your chances of experiencing a better outcome.

"Positive self-image is the
best preparation for success."
--Unknown

By no means, does preparing the best we can, mean that we will be guaranteed a positive outcome...there are too many variables, and this applies to both golf and life.

I'm just trying to emphasize that the **lack** of preparation, will breed less confidence and clutter your decision making process, both of which are critical elements on and off the course. We want to avoid this as much as possible. The outcome will be what it is, we should learn from it, and then move on.

And a very important factor in all of this is, you must practice with purpose and make every effort to practice in a fashion that is similar to how you will play. Making those as similar as you can in your mind, will help you take your game to the course much more efficiently.

Some final thoughts and questions for you. In golf, have you ever stood over the golf ball and had self-talk that was filled with doubt or fear? Or you addressed the ball and your feet didn't feel right, or you got ready, looked up and had second thoughts because it didn't look like you were aiming correctly? Ever had a "checklist" of things you were thinking about before you swung and going to try do all those in a few short seconds, once motion started? Find yourself being too attached to the outcome? Ever felt like you were hitting the ball great on the range and when you got to the first tee, everything changed?

In life, have you ever been in the middle of a party you are hosting and found yourself not enjoying the moment because you were not prepared enough? Ever found yourself racing with the clock, finishing up housecleaning before your guests ring your doorbell? Have a deadline at work or school and didn't prepare enough for, and feel the lack of confidence necessary to do a good job or get a good grade?

If you can say yes to any of those questions, or others you can think of, then it might be good time to re-evaluate your preparation steps.

"Golf is the closest game to the game we call life. You get bad breaks from good shots; you get good breaks from bad shots—but you have to play the ball where it lies."
--Bobby Jones

Remember the formula I shared with you earlier? **Potential − Interference = Performance!** It's very real and it can be managed by YOU! By listening to self-talk audio statements, you can re-wire your brain to start recreating your new reality in golf and in life.

Get ready by being more prepared, decrease your interference with good choices, and appreciate your golf game and your life at a whole new level. Reaching more of your full potential is exhilarating and waiting for you...are you ready? It's a great time to make a change and experience how preparation can give you confidence.

GOLF LESSON FROM CHAPTER 3

To be prepared, means you are ready for anything that comes your way. Prepare for each shot the best you can, prepare for the bounces, the luck, and the outcome. If you expect it, you can accept it. It's all part of the game, but being prepared increases your percentages of a positive outcome.

LIFE LESSON FROM CHAPTER 3

If you're prepared for life situations, there is much less risk for stress. Preparation is one of the key factors in our self-confidence and offers us the opportunity for success and growth. If you practice this on a regular basis, you will likely experience more good luck. Good luck is a remnant of preparation. And as they say… "Luck favors the prepared!"

PERSONAL REFLECTION AND INSIGHTS FROM CHAPTER 3

_____
_____
_____
_____
_____
_____
_____
_____
_____
_____
_____
_____
_____
_____

Chapter 4

EXPECTATIONS

"Past is experience, Present is experiment,
Future is expectation. Use your experience
in your experiment to achieve your expectation."
--Unknown

Irony struck when I wanted to start writing this chapter, I was at a complete stand still! I remember when I finished and submitted the chapter previous to it, I decided on what topic was next, and in the moment I wanted to begin, there was very little energy in my soul for how to commence.

I then had an epiphany... I was so excited about the chapter on "expectations" because I was expecting it to be one of the easier ones to write about, and it turned out to not necessarily be the case. Ahhh, the irony exposed, and one of the lessons from expectations we can learn...sometimes, if they are too high, it can unknowingly develop into a temporary setback.

It took some additional, more reflective time to think about the message I wanted to send to you, and then suddenly, "expectations" took on a life of its own. In the beginning of the journey, I found it was predominantly feeling like the concept was coming from such a negative perspective, and that is certainly not the message I wanted to convey. So I re-evaluated and let the universe sort through my thoughts to make sure they were in order with more clarity to share with you.

In my own discovery with this, through self-talk and sifting through the meaning of expectations in golf and life, was that we really have multiple ways for us to look at them. The only confusion for me was, I was looking at this from only one angle, and not from another point of view. The two I'm referring to are expectations from achievement and also from a relational aspect.

When that became evident, palpability entered and I could begin to articulate the message. Of course, because this is a book on golf and life, it will certainly play its role in both of these areas. Let's take a look at this from the golfing world, from both with my experiences as a player, and as an instructor with my students.

Looking back, when I was competing with very specific goals in mind, I am certain that my expectations were in alignment with how much I practiced and played, relative to the mechanical aspect of my game. As I have said before though, I did not have any type of mental game techniques to practice, so in truth, my expectations could not be applied realistically, to the total package of my game. It is necessary to prepare in both areas for peak performance, both physical and mental.

This ultimately, was my demise and became a huge obstacle of subconscious self-sabotage for me. I remember having very high expectations of myself for a good performance, because of how much time I put in on the practice range and course.

When I didn't come close to reaching some of them, I became exceedingly frustrated and thought I had failed on every level. Failed myself, my family, my community, my coach, everyone who was watching to see how I did. My self-esteem as a golfer and a person was very low, and peak performance is improbable in that type of situation.

"Achievement is largely the product
of steadily raising one's level
of aspirations and expectations."
--Jack Nicklaus

Today, with what I know now, I realize that I didn't fail at all, but in the moment, I certainly believed I had. Regrettably, I consistently repeated the negative thoughts and doubts in my head and with these programs, as it always does, it eventually became my reality. Sadly, I did not have an instructor that gave me direction as to how to deal correctly with the adversity that was inevitable on the golf course, and it is so important. I firmly believe this is a huge void in the golf instruction world today.

My practice sessions were filled with adverse self-talk, and my awareness of the damage negative thinking was having on my game was there, I just didn't know how to fix it. I was a living example of not having the 'missing link.' With that particular piece missing, it wasn't realistic that I could have my expectations as high as they were, due to the fact that my own self-talk was such a detriment to me and my game, and not my ally.

Fortunately, for you and many other golfers in the world, things are different now. I witness every single day, the evidence that supports my conclusion that golfers are not paying enough attention to the mental side of the game. It starts with taking an inventory of how much you do or do not pay attention to your own self-talk…what are you saying to yourself?

This negative thinking and a sense of defeat, happened to me, tournament after tournament, and after being completely battered and worn down enough, I finally just decided that competitive golf was "not for me." And thus, I gave up on my dreams in the amateur golfing world.

I transitioned into my professional career and my most lofty goal there, from a competitive perspective, was to win the annual LPGA Midwest Section Tournament in the Teaching and Club Professional membership. I came close a couple of times, but again, my self-talk demons were in my head, and I could not achieve my expectations, because the 'missing link' was still missing…the positive self-talk tool.

As a teacher, often, while I am giving a lesson, I hear my students reprimand themselves for not performing well. In that specific moment, I will stop and consider all of the factors involved and decide if it is a valid criticism. Sometimes it is, but usually it is not, and when I bring this to their attention, it becomes clear how their expectations don't meet their level of play or their preparation, during this time of their learning curve.

Let me give you an example. Recently, I had a student who just took up the game and thought that after only a month or so of lessons, he should be hitting the ball much further and more consistently than he was. So my question to him was, how much he had practiced in the last couple weeks, on my suggestions from the lessons. Here comes the real truth…little to none. *Maybe* only an hour or so of practicing each week, because he was too busy with other things… "life happened" as they say.

I asked this gentleman, that if he were to attempt to teach me something having to do with his occupation, how often would I need to practice the skills and apply the techniques, for me to get somewhat efficient at it?

Would I need to come to his workplace every day? Or. could I just show up for an hour a week and hope I can accomplish the task he was trying to teach me, without doing any application of the skills during the time in between when I last saw him? And, if I came only an hour a week, what should my expectations be of myself? The answer is pretty obvious, that my learning curve is going to be quite lengthy.

"The quality of our expectations
determines the quality of our actions.
--Andre Godin

He confirmed with me, that if I only showed up an hour a week, my learning curve would be very lengthy and I shouldn't expect to learn the skill very quickly. ***Exactly*** *my point!!* You cannot expect to practice only an hour a week and come to the next lesson with the idea you will be consistent and learn this game quickly.

There's just too much to learn in this game, it's not realistic, and it's likely not going to happen.

Remember, changing your habits with regards to anything requires repetition. If you don't, then the habit will not be mastered and will not remain. May I remind you that this applies to both the physical and mental aspects of the game.

I jokingly refer to my "magic sprinkle dust" that I can occasionally distribute to my students, but really, it's about teamwork and setting expectations that are sensible, realistic, and apply to where you are with your game and where you want to go.

Now, believe me, I understand completely how life can get ahold of you and there is little time to get everything completed in a day, especially at the pace of the 21st century. But, if you decide you want to take up the game of golf, or you want to improve you game, then it comes down to a matter of time blocking practice and playing on the course, in your calendar.

You really have no options with this, if you want to improve. You must realize your progress is directly proportionate to your practice and play, and your expectations should be in alignment with your efforts and intentions.

You simply cannot expect yourself to perform at a higher level if you do not put in the effort to learn the new habits. That only sets you up to think you are failing.

This can only lead to negative self-talk and improper programming for future progress. The potential consequences of this are; you may play frustrating golf a vast majority of the time, or worst case scenario, you'd quit playing the game all together.

Another point I want to make sure you are aware of is, practice time and playing on the course are two completely different things. When practicing, you are intentionally focusing and giving your attention to whatever you learned, to begin bridging the gap between old habits and creating new ones.

This takes repetition and focus, so when it comes time to applying it on the golf course, you do not have to think about it, you can be on auto pilot, be in the moment, and simply perform. Basically, you are ridding yourself of old programs or habits to establish new ones through repetition.

When you go on the course to play, this is where you play golf with joy, do not emotionalize your shots, take in the data, and upon completion, objectively evaluate your round, so you know what needs your attention in future practice sessions.

Let's take a look at this concept in a couple other sports like basketball and football for, for instance. The team practices all week to prepare for the games on the weekend. Having been a high achieving basketball player myself, I can tell you that our coach did not give us a specific plays or defenses to learn one day in practice, and expect us to go out the same day or the next night and execute them well.

We rehearsed these plays many, many times before we took our skills into real conditions, to see how they would work. Golf is no different, you must take a specific part of your game, learn to practice the skill and then take it to the course, evaluate, re-adjust and practice, then start the process over, again and again.

This idea of practicing properly applies to your mental game as well. You must learn how to "think" positively while practicing, and "think" positively while playing, so you minimize your stress levels and the mental anguish that you may experience during a round.

This is vastly overlooked by most golfers, and a huge missing piece of the puzzle for your progress and enjoyment of the game. Implementing both practice and playing to the physical *and* mental parts of your game with positive self-talk, is the secret sauce to your success. Not many golfers realize it or actually implement it.

If there hasn't been enough practice time, your old programs or habits are much stronger and you will default to them every single time…remember, the ***strongest program always wins.***

You need both, don't get me wrong, you simply must understand that they both require a different amount of attention and focus, to reach your goals and meet your expectations for your game. Practice is practice with repetition, whether it be block practicing or random, and playing is playing with evaluation and assessing what needs your attention.

"The only expectations you should live
up to are the ones you expect of yourself."
--Unknown

Golf is an acquired skill that takes time to learn with intentional practice, both on the physical and mental sides of the game, it simply cannot be a one-sided approach.

Golf is not a sprint, but more of a marathon when learning or improving your game...so please, make sure your expectations are realistic and in alignment with where you are on your learning curve. It's the only fair thing you can do for yourself, while you revel in playing one of the greatest games ever.

The other common mistake I see my students make is when they compare themselves to others, including the greatest players in the world, as they watch them on TV. I encourage you to watch their form and technique, as that will always be advantageous, and you no doubt will learn something.

It's when you start to compare their abilities to yours and you expect your game to be at a level similar to their game, that the disconnect occurs. Or you expect to "look like them," it's like comparing apples to oranges, it's not fair to yourself. You can try to emulate their swing, but remember, your physical stature may play a part in that as well.

These professionals practice with great intensity many hours a day, play consistently every week, and *it's their job!* Unless you are following a similar schedule, then it is more of a hobby for you.

For some golfers, it may be a serious hobby, with a rigorous practice and playing schedule, but either way, approach it with realistic expectations. This will enhance your experiences and keep things on a positive track. Raise your expectations accordingly, as you improve, and you will find yourself feeling satisfied with your progress.

In an article online at usgolftv.com by Troy Klongerbo he shared some interesting statistics based on expectations and why golfers need to keep them realistic.

He gave three reasons why amateur golfers should not get angry on the course, and defines the behavior as, "unreasonable self-abuse!" This is a perfect description of what some golfers do to themselves.

I pose questions to you after the statistics stated below, to grant you time to consider your expectations about your game, analyze all three valid points, and allow you to put things into perspective:

1.) On average, approach shots from 50-125—the BEST on the PGA tour was 15' 6" in 2014.

So I ask you…why are you so upset when you hit the green, but don't get "close enough?"

2.) Average putts made from 5-10 feet—the BEST on the PGA tour averaged 32% in 2014.

So I ask you…why are you so upset when you miss this length of a putt?

3.) 52 PGA players average less than 285 yards per drive in 2014.

So I ask you…why are you not pleased with an acceptable drive which you can easily play, relative to your current game?

To further make this point, here are some additional statistics that will be interesting for you to see. In 2014, these were the stats from the PGA tour on putting and percentages. They made:

1.) 99% of putts 3 feet and in
2.) 69% of 6 foot putts
3.) 54% of 8 foot putts
4.) 31% of putts between 10-15 feet

These statistics suggest the questions to you: How much are you expecting from yourself relative to those specific lengths of putts? Are you being realistic about it? Do the above statistics with either part of the game, surprise you at all?

When I share them with someone on the lesson tee, it generally raises some eyebrows. Why? Because students suddenly realize their expectations may well have been incongruent with the level of golfer they are at the moment. They began to realize they were thinking they should make more putts than high level golf professionals.

Looking at those objectively, you may need to start immediately managing and adjusting your expectations, relative to the level of your game. This will definitely improve your self-talk to a more positive mode and you will find yourself enjoying the moment much more.

If you haven't played or practiced much, then just go out and enjoy yourself, laugh, take in the moment; it's not the end of the world if you miss the green or don't make that putt! If you don't like how you are playing, fine tune your practice and playing time schedule and skills accordingly, to allow yourself the better to meet your expectations.

Now let's take a look at expectations relative to life. This is a bit trickier, because life and relationships are so complex, and when we add into the mix our own expectations, it can become even more tangled and difficult to process. We can have expectations of ourselves, others, the day, the universe, God, a higher power…. pretty much anything that we can think of. We might expect something of them, and if they don't come through or our expectations are not met, disappointment can result.

When you think about it, disappointment is a pretty heavy word. Disappoint means "to fail to fulfill the expectations or wishes of, to defeat the fulfillment of (hopes, plans, etc.); thwart; frustrate." I feel heavy when I read this definition, so understandably, if and when our expectations have not been fulfilled, we can feel that heavy or sad sensation.

Over the years, I certainly have disappointed myself at times, and I am sure I have disappointed others as well. But what I now know about self-talk and how it can help me through any of the issues I face, I feel like I have armor to protect me from negative forces. It is something I can rely on 100% of the time, my expectations of positive self-talk will always reward me.

"Your horizons have already
been expanded—you just have
to adjust your eyesight."
--Dr. Shad Helmstetter

By practicing and applying positive self-talk, and thinking differently, I can cope with things a lot better, setting my own personal expectations. I no longer compare myself to anyone else, because I am completely happy with who I am. I finally have found the 'missing link' that will improve my quality of life.

Whenever I feel disappointment, I make every attempt to look at it objectively and see if there was anything from my perspective that set it up in the first place. Did I contribute to the situation and, if so, how can I make it better the next time around. What can I do to improve? I look at where my expectation level was and adjust, if necessary. As mentioned, there have been times when I have been disappointed in myself, my students and others, but maybe I just expected too much.

I have to think about it a bit more often and be realistic regarding their progress. Odds are, they are simply working with their old programs and haven't had the opportunity to practice positive self-talk to reach their full potential. They may be doing the very best they can with the resources they have had, up to this point in their lives.

We should always have some sort of expectations from ourselves and others, but if they become too high, unreasonable, or too much from our own personal slant, then discord can result. I know from experience, that if people can sit down and simply talk things through, listen to the expectations of our loved ones, see things differently through the eyes of someone else, and observe how their world operates, peace and harmony will be much more attainable.

As Lao Tzu said, (taking it a step further) "Act without expectation" and if we exercise that thought, I believe our lives would take on a higher level of quality. It takes patience and understanding. You will better understand yourself and others, the previous programming you have both had, and be more apt to forgive and honor the spirit within.

Therein lies the reason I am *so* excited about sharing the 'missing link' with you, regarding both golf and life! Sometimes, when we release expectations, it gives us freedom to enjoy things for *what* they are, people for *who* they are, and not what we expect them to be.

This is a representation of simply "being present" in the universe and letting the moment unfold. With positive self-talk we are much more apt to let this happen, and our expectations and efforts are in alignment with each other, and comparing ourselves to others will be a thing of the past.

> *"You cannot change other people…*
> *only your expectations."*
> *--Unknown*

From a personal level, setting expectations for achieving something in life is always fun and challenging. Positive self-talk is an essential key to this, when striving to meet your expectations during the process. If and when you experience self-defeating messages, then it is very likely your goals and potential will be jeopardized

By setting yourself up with realistic goals coupled with positive self-talk, you create a solid platform for meeting the expectations you set. To do something remarkable, set some remarkable expectations! Give yourself the very best chance you can to succeed…you owe it to yourself, it's your gift.

GOLF LESSON FROM CHAPTER 4

No matter what level of golfer you are, you will have certain expectations of yourself as a player. Keep them congruent with the amount of time and effort you put into it and you will find yourself enjoying the game much more. Be fair, be patient, be realistic. If you expect it, then you can accept it.

LIFE LESSON FROM CHAPTER 4

The only person you should have expectations for is yourself. You control the choices you make and how far in life you want to go, but you can't make choices for others…it is their life to create, just as yours is for you to do as well. Keep your expectations positive, realistic, and steady and you will be a much happier person.

Be kind to yourself and know that when you expect too much of yourself, including perfection, you are likely going to become frustrated. Not being too hard on yourself is the first positive step towards being at peace. I saw a banner recently online that said, "I never thought I was a bully until I heard how I speak to myself. I think I owe myself an apology." So, if you are one of those people who needs to apologize to yourself, now is the time.

I had a student say to me on the lesson tee one night, "I am so nice to everybody else, why wouldn't I be nice to myself?" That is really a serious question and one I would encourage you to ponder.

PERSONAL REFLECTION AND INSIGHTS FROM CHAPTER 4

_____
_____
_____
_____
_____
_____
_____
_____
_____
_____

Chapter 5

IMPACT

*"Caring about others, running the
risk of feeling and leaving an impact
on people, brings happiness."
--Harold Kushner*

I will never forget back in 1984 when I attended my first golf school as a serious golfer and met a PGA professional by the name of Dr. Gary Wiren, who was one of the instructors. He was, and still is, very influential in the golfing industry and it was an honor to meet a legend in the teaching world.

During the golf school, I discovered he sold teaching aids and there was a specific one he endorsed, called the Impact Bag. This particular product was created to help you succeed in getting into a better impact position, and in his marketing and advertising, he referred to the impact position as "the moment of truth."

The irony came when I realized what an impact it made on my mind, when he was trying to make the point of how important this "moment of truth" actually was. To this day, I use this teaching aid on my own lesson tee, when trying to help my students feel the significance of impact.

Honestly, of all of the chapters in this book, this one holds a pretty special place in my heart. Upon reflecting on the dual purpose of words, I concluded that impact may have the most revering emotion when it comes to my passion and the message I want to convey.

Every single day while I am teaching, I strive to help a student achieve more efficient impact, no matter what the level of golfer they are. When a person contacts me and wants to learn the game of golf, the first order of business, after they understand the fundamentals, is to achieve contact with the golf ball, followed by direction, and then distance. So for contact in general, it's quite obvious that they need to be able to achieve an accomplished impact position.

With contact being one of the first priorities in the golfer's journey, it's pretty critical that we address it right away. It is very challenging on a golfer's mindset, when starting to learn how to play and in their attempt to hit the ball, they miss it completely, or in golfing terms, they "whiff" it.

When this happens, their self-talk will put them in a negative place very quickly, and if it continues, they could start to program themselves by saying, "I miss the ball all the time!" which is detrimental to their belief patterns and progress.

"Impact in golf...not an option, a necessity."
--Unknown

With a bit of humor in the mix, when one stops to think about what it really takes to impact a golf ball, I wonder if anyone would actually take the game up! As an instructor, I do want to make sure I articulate the task (sometimes daunting) of hitting a golf ball that is only 1.68" in diameter on the surface area of a golf club head (which is not much bigger, by the way), trying to hit it into a hole that is only 4.25" in diameter hundreds of yards away, while swinging on a circular plane, at a high rate of speed, with wrist activity, body turning, and weight shifting.

Whew!!! That was my fun way of telling golfers that this acquired skill may take some time, but for those of us who love golf, we know it's all worth it! I once heard one of my golf instructors say the golf swing is a "flat foot twist, with a closed face scrape, on the inside dimple, with discipline!" There are many ways to describe the golf swing, and smooth should be one of them.

I am sure you can you imagine some of the thoughts going through one's head, when you stop and think about what we are actually trying to do when we play this intricately balanced and unique game. No wonder golfers talk to themselves, and when they do, it is my goal that they are saying something positive, instead of negative thinking that can bring their morale down and program their thoughts incorrectly.

I tell my students that making contact with the golf ball is considered somewhat of a luxury. Failure to accomplish proper impact position, could quite possibly be called an epidemic in the golfing world. I hear it all the time from golfers, stating they want more consistency in their contact with the ball. I tell people that if I had a dollar for every time I heard that, I would have a nice little slush fund going!

It's no secret, impact will indeed have an enormous amount of importance to the quality of your game and how much fun you have. After all, if one doesn't achieve impact, or achieves partial impact, then the ball does not advance as well as you'd like, if at all, and frustration can settle in very quickly, thus the wrong programming with self-talk.

After some introductory conversation when a new student comes to the lesson tee, I always feel bad when I have to ask them to warm up and allow me to take a look at their swing before I start with instruction. One does not have to be a rocket scientist to know there is quite a bit of anxiety present and I am sensitive to the fact that I am making them feel vulnerable.

I literally can feel the tension, and anxiousness in their soul. Unintentionally, my presence is making an impact on their thoughts in this very moment. I apologize and they understand, but we both know it has to be done in order to get started.

Standing in front of a golf professional whom they just met, attempting to hit the ball, and then miss or top it time after time, is not a good feeling! I am guessing that's all they are praying for in that brief moment, is IMPACT…that's it!   Please…just let me *hit the ball!* Sometimes that can be quite a colossal request under the circumstances, but in the end, it's all for the good of their improvement.

I wish I could tape their self-talk though! I sometimes do hear it, because they will, without even knowing it, talk out loud verbalizing their thoughts and expressing their fear. Or, they confess to me later how nervous they were during that time.

During the process, one of the most common remarks someone will make after they've missed the ball completely is "There, I always do that!" I realize their negative self-talk is on high alert now and they are filled with fear and anxiety. I can empathize with them, as I have done it myself more times than I want to remember over the years, believe me.

A personal example of this for me was back in my amateur days, and I must admit it was hands down, one of my most humiliating moments in my golfing career. It didn't happen on the lesson tee, and not in any typical tournament, but in a national USGA Mid-Amateur event in Austin, Texas.

I had a professional golfer caddying for me (he now plays on The Champions Tour.) As I was on about the 8th hole, I stepped up to the tee box, executed my pre-shot routine, took the club back, swung through and *whoosh!* Wouldn't you know it…I almost whiffed the ball with my 3-wood. It ended up only about 2-3 inches in front of my tee! I was devastated and my self-talk was filled with everything from self-doubt, fear and anxiety to complete panic!

It was bad enough that I felt like I was having an out-of-body experience and wanted to run and hide under a rock...but the truth was, I had to gather my thoughts and try to hit that little white ball again, with the confidence of a teenager on his/her first day of high school. How could I have done that? How embarrassing is that? I can't believe I am that stupid! How many people saw me do that? What do I do now? Oh my gosh, I hope I don't do it again....and the list of negative comments went on and on. The rest of my round was not too pretty after that point.

Have you ever swung at a golf ball and missed it? Do you have any recollection of how that made you feel? Chances are at some point in time, most, if not all golfers, can claim that they have whiffed the golf ball. It can be one of the fastest ways to generate some of the most chaotic internal dialogue that is filled with uncertainty, known to humankind, if we do not achieve impact, even partial impact, when that's what you are trying to achieve!

If you haven't experienced vulnerability on the golf course before, once you experience poor impact, you will most definitely feel it then. I remember telling somebody one time early in my golfing life, "At least you hit the ball all the time, even if you don't know where it's going. I can't even do that!" Impact with your club face and the golf ball is not only critical to your enjoyment of the game...it's essential!

On the flip side of not achieving impact, let's take a look at what we experience when impact is precise and perfect. I have heard many times; a golfer say that it was the last great shot on the 18th hole that "brings them back again" for another round. Yes, indeed! A well-struck golf ball will be one of the most sought after achievements a golfer will ever strive for.

I have students that have told me that they would rather shoot a higher score and hit the ball better, than to have a lower score and hit it poorly. I am sure this concept can be challenged by some of you, but truthfully speaking, precision is really what golf is about, and I do understand their mindset when it comes to this thought process.

One day while teaching, when a student hit a shot dead center in the middle of the club face, I stopped and asked him, "How did that feel?" His response surprised me at first, but then after thinking about it, it made complete sense. He answered by saying, "I didn't feel anything at all!" You see, if we hit the center and achieve proper impact, we will not feel any vibrations, and it is the shot I just referred to in the previous paragraph, that brings us back to play once again! Centeredness of contact is one of the ball flight laws, so obviously, it is quite important.

When this happens, the golf club, ball, and you the golfer, are in complete synchronicity with one another. A miss-hit shot on the other hand, will send nasty vibrations traveling up the golf shaft, into our hands, arms and shoulders creating a very bad sensation for the golfer, sometimes pain, and most likely a bad shot.

So, what do I encourage my students to do after they have not reached a preferred impact position? There are many drills and concepts to convey the message, but a couple that are quite effective are having them swing in slow motion and stop at impact position, to see what their clubface and hands look like. I also have a drill called the "impact drill" that encourages them to practice the position more efficiently, with a short abbreviated swing accentuating impact position.

When it comes to impact in our daily life, there always seems to be plentiful opportunities for us to make a positive impact. I can tell you that from a very early age, I have always wanted to make a positive impact on people's lives, and as I get older, it is becoming an increased passion of mine. With deep gratitude, I have come to realize that I have been able to give back to others while being on the lesson tee as an instructor, giving one-on-one private lessons.

Golf was the vehicle that allowed me to help people and make them feel good about themselves, achieve goals and enjoy the sport--and what a gift it has been for me! But there was something that was speaking even deeper in my heart and sending messages to me, saying the impact I was going to make through golf was to be considerably more meaningful in the near future…far beyond my wildest dreams.

"Could anything be better than this?
Waking up every day knowing that lots
of people are smiling because you
chose to impact lives, making the
world a better place!"
--Anyaele Sam Chiyson

I listened to that still small voice inside my head talking to me every day, telling me to take a chance and trust my intuition, and most of all have courage to go out and make a positive impact on the world.

The single most influential thought that changed everything for me was what my mother taught me early in life. She always told me that if I wanted to feel good about myself, then I needed to do something nice for others. What a profound yet simple concept to follow, and it works like magic! In addition to that idea, I also knew that if I wanted something to change, then *I* must change…so I did!

It was when I intentionally started to take action and follow my heart, that my company Gratitude Golf, LLC came into existence. Don't get me wrong, it wasn't that I didn't appreciate and cherish every moment that I have had, teaching people golf, but I knew I wanted to give back on a grander scale, I wanted to make a bigger impact on the world.

When I started to *live* gratitude instead of talking about gratitude, my life took on more meaning and the paradigm of my world changed forever. I often wonder how amazing it would be if everyone during their busy day, would just stop and share one positive expression or gesture to another person with whom they crossed paths. I believe we would suddenly realize what kind of impact one makes on another, and how wonderful and more positive this world would be! I love how Robin Williams puts the idea of impacting the world by saying… "YOU CAN CHANGE THE WORLD, no matter what people tell you, words and ideas can change the world."

I have no doubt it would make a huge impact on people's attitudes if there was more positive energy flowing around the streets, in airports, while people are driving their cars, at large venues, at sporting events, in boardrooms, at colleges and universities, in the school systems, in hospitals, in homes all across the world... everywhere!

> *"Never underestimate the valuable*
> *and important difference you are in every*
> *life you touch. For the impact you make*
> *today has a powerful rippling effect*
> *on every tomorrow."*
> *--Unknown*

My husband and I have a dear friend who recently had a near-death experience. During a conversation with him, he shared a fascinating story with us about one of the things he remembers after "coming back", and it is the concept that "we are all intricately connected, the human race is in this together." We must consciously connect from a positive perspective to make this world a better place, and it's going to be up to us to make that choice.

Showing your positivity has been documented as being very contagious, just as it would be contagious having a negative attitude. The impact that you can have by just sharing a simple smile with someone when you're walking past them could be the difference between them having a really bad day, or you giving them hope that humanity is kind and loving.

Sometime, check out the video on YouTube called the "Laughing Tram Man." My guess is you will find yourself smiling very quickly! We all have our own stories and struggles every day, but with a kind gesture of a smile or giving back and paying it forward to someone, you could create a huge impact on their attitude moving forward.

Here's an example of being connected with someone through golf and showing compassion by listening and caring, and how it can generate a positive impact. One day on the lesson tee, I realized that my student wasn't needing a golf lesson as much as he needed to talk about some things and realize that he was full of tension and stress. So we stopped the lesson and just sat down and talked about his golf goals and his life, as it was at the moment.

It was after that particular lesson, that I had the opportunity to share the book *"What To Say When You Talk To Your Self"* by Dr. Shad Helmstetter, with him. Within a few weeks my student approached me with open arms, wanting to give me a hug, and said "Thank you so much for changing my life."

He shared that for months he had been experiencing a great deal of stress and pressure at work and at home. He texted me one night and said how ashamed he was that he had broken two of his golf clubs, ruined one of his laptops, and busted up a cooking apparatus. After I shared the book with him, he realized that his self-talk was impacting every facet of his life in an incredibly negative way, and he knew he had to change.

The impact that had resulted from the simple sharing of a book with a profound, foundational message, made all the difference in the world to this young man. He changed his self-talk and it has changed his life. He's enjoying golf more, now that he's relaxed and is aware of the tension he was carrying around.

"You cannot get through a single day without having an impact on the world around you. What you do makes a difference, and you have to decide what kind of difference you want to make."
--Unknown

He has set boundaries at work that have allowed him to let go of resentment and feel productive with confidence, and his life at home is more harmonious. His wife has also taken up golf, so they can do something enjoyable together. He created a better world for himself and his life, by changing how he was thinking and becoming more positive through listening to positive self-talk.

So, can one make an impact on somebody, by simply taking time to listen, sharing a smile, giving them a hug, greeting them, recognizing and validating their presence, noticing them in a positive way, and letting them know they matter? **ABSOLUTELY**!!

We have countless ways that we can share positivity in the world and make an impact on other people's lives each and every day, whether we know them or not. Any act of kindness, any words of encouragement, or any good deed shall not go unnoticed. The world needs this action more than ever these days, and we as human beings who were born to love, need to be vigilant in sharing peace and harmony with one another. I like the scripture that says, "Let us think of ways to motivate one another to acts of love and good works." Hebrew 10:24

How many times have you let your own self-talk, talk you right out of doing something positive for someone else? Did you ever have a complimentary thought you would like to share with someone, that could be as simple as "I like your shoes, where did you get them?" and then not express your thoughts to them?

Or, it could be a deeper thought such as "I love you" when thinking about how much you love someone, and then not sharing your feelings with them. Let your thoughts be loving, let your actions be kind, express your gratitude, and most of all, pay it forward when you can. I remember in my younger days, calling up my parents and getting them both on the phone at the same time, simply to say how much I loved them. I was thinking it, so I acted on my thoughts and conveyed my message. It made all the difference in the world to them at the time, and for me, it gave me a sense of peace and harmony that all is good.

"Service to others is the rent you pay
for your room here on earth."
--Mohammad Ali

When I started "living gratitude" daily in my life, one of the quotes that made an impression on me, was, "Unexpressed gratitude is like buying a present, wrapping it up, and then never giving it to the intended recipient." Make every effort to positively impact somebody's life today, as it could be the single most important thing you do for those who least expect it and may need it. It's just as important as the impact position is in golf.

IMPACT... the moment of truth... in golf and in life... it's essential and **YOU** can make the difference!

GOLF LESSON FROM CHAPTER 5

The moment of truth...when the ball is launched into airspace and its destiny and fate has now been determined. Solid impact is the essence of golf, so strive to achieve consistent impact with a relaxed swing, and you'll be a satisfied golfer.

LIFE LESSON FROM CHAPTER 5

Every day we have the opportunity to positively impact someone's life. If we wake up each and every day with this positive thought in mind, the world would indeed be a better place. You have this very gift to share. Open your heart, smile, notice others, and you'll become a light to others. Your intentional effort to want to make a difference, could turn someone's darkness into light.

PERSONAL REFLECTION AND INSIGHTS FROM CHAPTER 5

_____

_____

_____

_____

_____

Chapter 6

BALANCE

> *"Next to love, balance is the*
> *most important thing."*
> *--John Wooden*

Whether we know it or not, we are always talking to ourselves, much more than we realize. It's not until we start monitoring it, that one realizes how **much** and **what** is actually being said. When I discovered this, I came to the harsh reality that the majority of my self-talk was not in my favor and was working against me.

It was when I realized this that I could stop the negative and replace it with the positive to make it more balanced, and suddenly, the paradigm of my world shifted. This applied to both my personal life and my life on the golf course.

If I could have had more positive, balanced self-talk in my competitive golfing days, I am certain I would have reached many more of my desired outcomes and goals. The percentage of negative -vs- positive self-talk was *very* much out of balance.

How aware are you of your self-talk on and off the golf course? Is it helping you or hurting you? How many times a day do you say something to yourself that is criticizing your character and who you are? There is no time like the present to listen to what is being said and make some changes, if needed.

Balance...the elusive factor in one's life, that we may not recognize is gone until we stop and ask ourselves the question of "Why are things so stressful right now?" I have found through my own struggles in life, and when I feel overwhelmed, it forces me to stop and evaluate what is really going on, and I discover that I am simply out of balance with my priorities in life.

Both my personal and professional life have experienced imbalances, and when I chunk it down and analyze to restructure, I can see more clearly. I like one of the definitions I found for the word balance used as a noun; "mental steadiness or emotional stability, habit of calm behavior." What a *great* way to think about balance!

One of the most effective concepts to help me re-evaluate the situation and get back on track is this idea: There are certain things in life you can control and there are things in life you cannot control. Control the controllables. Take a look at the frustrating situations that you cannot control, and you'll realize you are likely fussing over nothing, because there is not a thing you can do about it anyway!

> *"Harmony is a beautiful balance*
> *between mind, body and soul,*
> *measured in tender, peaceful moments."*
> *--Melanie Koulouris*

What are some things in the game of golf or life that you cannot control but may be causing you stress and/or negative self-talk? How about in your family life, work, relationships with friends? Understand that the things you cannot control, should not be influencing your attitude. Make conscious decisions on the parts you can control, and if you need to change something, do so. Then…. move on…your slate is clean.

I remember back early in my career when I was fortunate enough to be asked to speak at an LPGA event in Michigan, and each of the speakers was given a single word to talk about. I had the luck of the draw, in my opinion, because I got the word "balance." In my preparation for the event, and as I was reflecting on how balance in golf and life are so similar, it brought forth a grace-filled speech, that was so easy to present and share with the audience.

It was a pleasure on all levels, as I enjoyed preparing for it, watching as people's eyes light up when I spoke, with heads nodding, and talking to people after the event, about how it made them think about their own balance at the moment. A pleasant reminder for me as well, to continue maintaining balance in my own life, both personal and professional.

It is a graceful (perhaps, "an intricate") dance to keep our lives flowing effortlessly and being in the moment. Our mindfulness or awareness of what we need to do, once we get off kilter, is the necessary step towards internal peace, which brings about a balanced feeling.

When I think of the word balance, one of the first things that comes to mind is harmony, having a sense of being in control (in a good way) and not experiencing too much chaos. Balance to me is such a metaphor for life, as I believe each of us yearns for it, it's just that when things get crazy, we realize things may have gotten out of hand and it's time to make some changes.

"The key to keeping your balance
is knowing when you lost it."
--Anonymous

As I mentioned earlier, for me, the first signal and red flag that I have come to an imbalanced place, is when I feel very overwhelmed with my experiences and can't deal with issues logically, it's more of an emotional reaction I'm operating from. This is when the amygdala fires up and takes over, which makes us "stupid" in our decision- making process, and this can be jeopardized immeasurably.

Our self-talk is negative, blaming is abundant, and the programming will not be favorable. It's not a preferred place to operate from, and we may experience some regrets, if we don't stay calm and then potentially make ill decisions. I have been in conversations with people where this happened, and believe me, it's best to just reconvene at a later time.

I know that when I become emotionally charged in a negative way, I have to take a serious look at what's on my platter. It's when I sit down, take a look in the mirror, and ask myself what is going on and what is my part, that I can start to see the path to clarity.

When I write things down on paper and see it right in front of me, the realization of imbalance becomes tangible. I then can sort through some of the issues I am facing, and make choices as to what stays and what goes; then I can begin to find peace and balance once again. I have simply prioritized and took action.

Pertaining to golf and an emotional reaction on the course, if you are out of balance emotionally in that environment, you will likely be indecisive or make bad decisions, which puts more mental anguish on yourself while you are playing, and cause scores to increase. It serves no purpose and only causes major interference, which is generally damaging to your experience overall. Decision making on the course is a key component in your game, so not emotionalizing your shots is very important.

Letting golf dictate your emotions off the course is also risky. Taking time to evaluate and know what needs work, is a much higher road to take. After the round, ask yourself what was good and what could be better. Even when focusing on what needs work, look at it from a positive frame of mind. Your score does not define who you are, so letting your emotions get out of control is not the path to improvement.

My granddaughter says it best when she says, "Grandma, that person is being rude rabbit!" I am sure some of us have experienced that, either way, being the golfer or the observer. The reality of it all is, "rude rabbits" are not fun to be around or play golf with. Keep your emotions in balance, and you, plus others, will benefit!

"Golf is a search for perfection, for balance.
It's about meditation and concentration.
You have to use hand and brain."
--Celine Dion

Something interesting to ponder…when we are angry and upset, our body chemically produces cortisol which stays with is much longer than we'd like, and it acts like a timed release capsule in our system. When we are happy and positive, our body produces oxytocin, which helps us through those tough times to stay more calm, and we are in better control of our emotions, not the adverse, where our emotions are in control of us.

I am quite certain that if I went back and could document all of the things that went through my mind while competing, the list would be daunting as far as how hard I was on myself, and how I completely set myself up to not reach some of my goals, even though I was not aware of it. I would have given anything to have the tool of self-talk and knowledge of neuroplasticity and re-wiring, to help me on my journey back then, and keep my thoughts in balance. It would have been a game changer for me.

Our mindfulness and the ability to listen to what we say to ourselves, is the first step to putting us back on track, to counteract the negative and make a change. How much do you say to yourself on the course or in your daily life that is negative and has a toxic effect on yourself, your presence with those around you, and to your intended outcome?

Staying balanced with both your swing and your mind is a conscious effort that takes some intentional work, but so worth it. The idea here of the 'missing link' as the tool to help you with that, is great news! What I know, having taught this game for so many years and painfully watching people out of balance, is that there is an indisputable connectedness between your thoughts and your game, and that your outcome is much more than your swing.

How important is balance? It basically stabilizes everything…it helps to bring back some sort of order and structure in a very crazy world that may have us living our day-to-day lives on autopilot and not even being aware of what may be making us feel really out of control or out of balance. Think of yourself walking a tight rope and how you will vacillate when you move too much to one side or the other. Once you find the center of your body, you will start to control your balance once again, and be back in the driver's seat.

In my profession on a seasonal basis, my life can take a direct hit of imbalance, when it comes to giving lessons. During the spring months and when the golfers get spring fever to get back out on the golf course, my lesson numbers will increase dramatically, and then during the fall and with winter fast approaching, my lessons decrease substantially. It's part of the lifecycle of golf instruction.

Don't get me wrong, this is a good problem to have. I love what I do, although, during my busy months when many people are requiring a large portion of my time, I must be very mindful that I do not let my life get too far out of balance, paying close attention that I don't become too busy to remember the very important things in my life.

Making sure I carve out time to spend with my family and friends and keeping track of my calendar with time blocking, is critical to my well-being, so I don't miss events that are very important to me. If we miss those precious moments and events, we cannot re-create them or bring them back, so it's essential we make arrangements to be present for all that we can be.

The fall of 2015, will be a perfect example of a "once in a lifetime moment" in my life. My youngest son, Nathan, was chosen as the 60th drum major for The Ohio State University Marching Band or lovingly known to many, as the Best Damn Band In The Land (TBDBITL).

I guarantee you I had already time blocked and carved out my calendar to be at every possible game, event, and function he is performing at, so I can create as many memories as I can and watch my son experience the pure joy from his hard work! The only way to do that is to make sure we are staying in balance and attentive to our calendar, create the time to be present.

WARNING…this time blocking exercise may offend some people when you have to tell them "no" to a request they may have, but ultimately, you know the right decision has been made. Remember, you can't bring these moments back. This is a great lesson in setting boundaries, to help you maintain balance in your life.

"Balance is not something you FIND,
it is something you CREATE."
--Jana Kingsford

Balance in the golf swing, on the other hand, is probably just as important as it is in your personal life. Back when I watched my coach teach young aspiring male golf pros who wanted to play on the tour, he would tell them he only wanted to have them swing to the power of eight.

What he meant by this is, don't swing so hard that you can't keep your balance, because this will lead to greater inconsistency. With a full swing, a balanced follow-through is one of the secrets. A consistent swing starts with a good, balanced finish!

An easy way to help these players achieve this was applying a thought of 1 to 2 and hold. Position #1 is your backswing, position #2 is your follow through, and then hold your finish until the ball lands. This requires balance of your body and centeredness.

This is how we taught our children to swing a golf club. Our oldest son Jay was the first to experience this concept, and I must say, I don't think I have **ever** seen him swing out of balance. Now at 6'3" tall, he has one of the longest swing arcs and most flowing swings I have ever seen, and he can hit it a country mile, all the while, staying in complete balance. Don't get me wrong, if you saw him swing, he does indeed swing hard, but he knows how maintain his balanced finish, and the sequence of his motion is repeatable. He is living proof that power can still have balance as one of the major components.

"The best quick tip in golf is to
focus on your rhythm and balance."
--Hale Irwin

Another example of this is, I most recently had a young man in his mid-twenties come to the lesson tee complaining that he had completely "lost his swing" from our last lesson. Now we all know that that is pretty hard lose it from one lesson to the next, especially at the level of golf he plays at because he is a single digit handicap player. But in his mind, it was a reality, thus it was reality!

For the most part, the lesson for him that day consisted of reminding him that the golf swing is a sequence of events called timing, and if you swing too hard and cannot keep your balance, then you will have great difficulty finding the ball on the face of the club with precision, because things did not happen in the right place.

I will often refer to timing on the lesson tee as the "Holy Grail of Golf," and in my opinion, by far one of the most difficult elements to teach a student. Anytime one is moving at 60-100+ miles an hour and expect precision to happen, it definitely falls under the category of an acquired skill. It takes timing, rhythm, and balance.

Balance used as a verb gives a nice connection to golf when it's defined as "a move forward and backward, or in opposite directions, and to bring to or hold in equilibrium, poise." So as it goes, we come to realize the old cliché might indeed be true that...timing is everything, in golf *and* in life!

> *"Life is a balance of holding*
> *on and letting go."*
> *--Rumi*

When we finally got his balance back, in his mind, the intensity with which he was swinging at was around a 4-5 on a scale of 10, but in reality, it was really closer to an eight. He felt like he was in slow motion, but he wasn't, it was just the right pace he needed to keep the sequence intact, and give him the best opportunity to achieve a balanced finished position. He was much more consistent with contact and direction, thus a much happier golfer.

There is a saying I use in golf and share with my students when one is pushing too hard to make something happen. The expression is "less is more" and in this case, it literally helped him regain balance. In all my years of teaching, 99.9999% of the students I have taught, want more consistency in their game, and to reiterate an all-important concept, **all consistent swings have a good balanced finish.**

Relative to practicing your golf game, you must also be mindful of balance. Knowing what your score consists of and where the strokes come from, will help you to create balance in what you practice. If you practice only certain areas or with certain clubs, you will have a disproportionate and non-purposeful practice session, and you will start to believe you dislike specific clubs or you are not good at a specific shot or area of your game.

If anyone ever tells me that they dislike a club, I immediately go and get that particular club out of their bag and say, "OK then, let's start getting to know your new best friend!"

I have a saying I repeat every now and again, and it goes like this, "If you don't like a shot, practice it a lot." Likewise, if someone mentions an area of the game they very much dislike, i.e. the bunker and never practice it, we are soon taking a trip to the sand! Balancing out what you practice, the clubs you practice with and how many hours a week you practice, will be essential to your progress.

So taking time to look at balancing your self-talk on the golf course, and in the course of your daily lives, will undoubtedly determine the level of your enjoyment and the quality of your experience, in both cases. We can talk ourselves into any type of situation, knowing whatever we are saying and repeating, will indeed become the strongest program, thus our reality. Because as we know, *the strongest program always wins.*

> *"The best and safest thing is to keep balance*
> *in your life, acknowledge the great powers around*
> *us and in us. If you can do that, and live that way,*
> *you are really a wise man."*
> *--Euripides*

So is your self-talk balanced or imbalanced? Are you even aware of what you are saying to yourself during the day or in the moment? I hear students every day on the lesson tee talk out loud, and it is predominantly negative comments about what they think they can't do, serving the negativity of their outcome. This imbalance of our self-talk is something that every instructor should be addressing to meet the needs of the students to help them improve their game.

Golfers are very quick to scold themselves and very slow to praise. They believe they can't hit a specific shot and then proclaim, "See, I told you I can't hit that shot!" This is nothing but self-prophecy folks, your thoughts are out of balance, in a negative way. You continue to believe you can't hit a specific shot, and it will become reality soon enough.

When someone achieves a goal on the lesson tee, I have a powerful anchor or way of affirming their efforts, and it makes them smile every time I ask them to do it. At first, I witness them feeling a bit awkward and hesitating, but in time, they are doing it on their own.

I tell them right after the accomplishment, this is a "right hand to left shoulder" moment! Meaning, they must take their own right hand and pat themselves on the left shoulder, giving themselves an affirming gesture, a positive anchor, and praising themselves! This is the beginning of the path to becoming our own best friend!

Can you imagine it being difficult giving yourself a pat on the back and giving praise for doing something right? Seems hard to believe, but it is true. You would pat someone else on the back if they achieved something, wouldn't you? This action is a great way to keep balance, in order to offset those comments that are not life giving and work against you. And, guess what? It just might make you smile!

In an article titled The Ideal Praise-to-Criticism Ratio written by Jack Zenger and Joseph Folkman in the Harvard Business Review, it was stated that "Only positive feedback can motivate people to continue doing what they're doing well, and do it with more vigor, determination, and creativity. Perhaps that's why we have found with the vast majority of the leaders in our database, who have no outstanding weaknesses, that positive feedback is what motivates them to continue improvement."

> *"Life is like riding a bicycle. To keep your balance,*
> *you must keep moving." –Unknown*

Why would we not want to be our own best friends in life, on and off the course? Why is it that we are so nice to others, but not to ourselves? Is it time for you to take a look in the mirror and discover how your positive or negative self-talk is influencing your outcome? Is the self-talk in your life and with your golf game on the course, helping our hurting you?

It's never too late to take an inventory and make a change…you'll be glad you did! Find your own personal balance and you will tap into a much more resourceful YOU! Enjoy your new life of balance…

GOLF LESSON FROM CHAPTER 6

All consistent golf swings, have a good balance to finish. In golf, there's a saying that "less is more" and if you remain in balance, your swing will render a desired outcome more often. Remember, 1 to 2 and hold your finish until the ball lands, is a great way to practice balance. And, maintain positive self-talk on the course to keep your internal compass in a peaceful, balanced place.

LIFE LESSON FROM CHAPTER 6

We can always find ourselves "too busy" with our lives and feel there's not enough time in the day to get things done. Find a nice balance between work, family/friends, and pleasure. Stop and take time to enjoy the little things in life and express your gratitude when the opportunity presents itself. Realize what really matters in your life and do more of that. Don't miss out on what is truly important in your life, those times define the quality of the dash in between your first breath and your last. And when you stop to look in the mirror at yourself, realize that the person you are looking at is enough, and you are all that you need to be in that very moment…you are beginning to find balance.

PERSONAL REFLECTION AND INSIGHTS FROM CHAPTER 6

_____

_____

_____

_____

_____

_____

_____

_____

_____

_____

_____

_____

_____

_____

Chapter 7

AWARENESS

> "When I need, I plan. When I'm down, I trust.
> When I stumble, I get help. When I doubt, I have faith. When
> I'm unsure what to do next, I keep going.
> When I succeed, I share."
> --Dr. Shad Helmstetter

It was a day in early August, when I asked my son, Nathan and his fiancée Chrissy, to come over for dinner that evening. My intent was to give Nathan the gift of a golden whistle I had purchased at a silent auction, as a symbol of his being the "leader of the band" and one he might possibly use during a game in his 2015 season as drum major.

Unexpectedly, after I gave him the gift, he promptly said to me... "Well, I have something for you too!" He informed me he had arranged for a ticket for me to go to London, England to watch the Ohio State Marching Band perform at an NFL game in Wembley Stadium for the first time in history, and he really wanted me to be a part of the excitement.

It was in that very moment, that the awareness level of my fear began to rise, as I started to think about the fact that I really was going to travel out of the country...by myself. There's no backing out now! I remember the visceral feeling I had when they told me I was definitely going, the reservation was already made, and they were going to send me the itinerary. Multiple thoughts were racing through my mind.

First and foremost, I was hoping my fear wasn't obvious to them and potentially thwarting the excitement and generosity Nathan and Chrissy were feeling, by gifting me this opportunity. I certainly did not want to be rude and was overwhelmed by the thoughtfulness.

In a split second, I was literally saying to myself that I am not sure I can, or even want to do this. I began to think of reasons why I wouldn't accept this gracious gift, or if I did go, what other people I might be able to talk into going with me, so I would not have to go alone. How about my mother? She loves to travel, maybe I could talk her into going with me, or my daughter Erin, maybe she'd find time on her calendar to be my traveling partner. Certainly, someone would accompany me, so I didn't have to embark on this alone. And all the while, I couldn't help ponder as to why this was striking such fear in my heart.

Over the next few days and weeks and with a bit of trepidation, I renewed my passport, prepared in my mind to take the trip, and had time to process what was imminent…I was traveling by myself to London, England. In reality, I definitely wanted to be a part of history to watch my son perform, and see my sister and brother-in-law. Over time, I began to get excited about what I was going to see and experience. I felt a great sense of gratitude that Nathan allowed me the opportunity to go, and of course, the bonus was, I was going to be able to visit family.

It has been twenty plus years that my sister Elizabeth has lived overseas, and for the last ten years she's been living in London. For as long as I can remember, she has invited me to come and visit and see her part of the world. And for whatever reasons, all of those years, I have declined and come up with what I felt were justifiable "excuses" as to why I could not and would not travel across the pond.

In retrospect, and in time, I became aware of the real reason…I was actually quite scared to travel such a distance. I recalled my father's own attitude on travel. He never wanted to leave our hometown, let alone the country! He used to literally talk himself into becoming physically ill, if and when he ever left town, for anything other than a basketball game or tournament.

I even remember in the 70's he won a trip to Scotland from the insurance company he worked for, and he refused to go, so my mom took advantage of it anyway, went by herself, and of course, she had an amazing time.

"Developing an awareness of life beyond your immediate surroundings brings a healthy restlessness which, if infused with peace and used well, can be a foundation for positive change in the world."
--Dadi Janki

Back then, I thought my father's fear and behavior was totally ridiculous, and never thought I would be that way. But when I found out I was traveling to London by myself, I had a sense of what he was feeling when he was out of his milieu. I realized how he talked himself right into panic and sickness with his beliefs about traveling, and I definitely did not and would not follow that pattern. This trip for me, that I didn't plan, helped me to become aware of my own fears, and face them straight on. I was determined to do this, be grateful, and learn what I needed to learn and grow from the experience!

Why do I share this particular story with you? Because I found it so interesting and compelling how out of touch I was with my own awareness over the past twenty-some years, regarding my fear of not wanting to travel out of the country and stepping out of my comfort zone.

The thought of an eight-hour plane flight was daunting (even though I know for some people who travel a lot, that is probably a short flight), and I wondered…could I really do that, be 30,000+ feet up in the air, amidst a bunch of strangers in an airplane, cooped up for that long with nowhere to go? I don't sleep well on airplanes, I don't like being in confined spaces for any length of time, I'm a bit germ phobic, I am going to be exhausted. How do I even prepare for that?

Staring a very uncomfortable situation right in the face, over time, I began to tell myself this surely wasn't that big of a deal, lots of people do it every day. I can research how to prepare most efficiently to make the trip easier for me, and I concluded, I was being way too paranoid.

When I decided to change my self-talk, suddenly, my paradigm about the entire trip began to shift and change into a potentially positive event, instead of one I was nervous about. It was truly all about my thoughts and self-talk, and my decision to change my thoughts, changed my outlook, and ultimately changed my entire experience.

"The first step toward change is awareness.
The second step is acceptance."
--Nathaniel Brenden

The trip itself did wonders for reframing my fears and beliefs of my never wanting to leave the country. I found so many things to be grateful for while in England, and had to chuckle when I said to my sister one afternoon while I was over there, "I understand that we don't have time to see that tourist attraction now, but I will definitely have to see it when I come back on my next trip!"

What a change in my attitude from August to October, and it all had to do with how my thoughts and self-talk approached the situation. Thanks to the opportunity I was given by my son, I now have a broader look at the world. My awareness of the limitations my thoughts were putting on me, were the key to my progression of experiencing life on another level, and I saw London for real instead of from pictures in a book!

Whether it's a trip overseas, flying in a plane for longer than you can imagine, taking on a new job, daring to be different, having the courage to step out of your comfort zone, feeling vulnerable, just know that personal and professional growth always comes from these situations. Communicate more effectively with those you love, do something you have always dreamed of doing, but never thought you could…whatever it is…the main thing is to believe that you can do it!

Know that your self-talk and thoughts will either hold you back or propel you forward, it's all up to you. Your awareness of those thoughts will be what help you take the steps necessary to allow you to enjoy the experience, and it could change *everything!*

Awareness in your golf game is very similar. You must realize what you are or are not doing before you can begin to change your patterns. I find it fascinating when giving golf instruction, that awareness level of specific elements in a swing, are either high, moderate, or not at all. Most of the time, when the awareness level is non-existent, is when the student will have the biggest epiphanies and light bulbs come on.

When I bring something to your attention, you will suddenly become aware of the fact that you were not aware that you were doing something incorrectly! Another way to say this is, "You know that you don't know." Sounds kind of silly but true, and when the change is made, it's both surprising and enlightening and often produces positive results rather quickly.

Often, I have students tell me, "I had *no* idea I was even doing that!" In this very moment, you can discover that there might be something that has been holding you back from progress or playing the game at the level you are seeking, and you then become much more willing to change and create the new habit. As Eckhart Tolle so aptly put it, "Awareness is the greatest agent for change."

Bottom line, is the fact that when you are more aware of specific changes having to do with your game, then it heightens your ability for progress and you will be able to experience a breakthrough in your journey. It's the awareness and self-talk that will catapult your evolution and help you to reach your goals and full potential. This will apply to both body awareness and mental game awareness.

If you are a beginner golfer or have just started in the last couple of years, being mindful of the fact that there is a great deal of information to learn about golf, will be very helpful. Knowing this going into the learning process, prepares you for it, thus you will have more patience.

Over the years in my teaching, I came up with a statement you can categorize as food for thought, to help you be more aware in your quest to acquire the skill of golf. I like to tell my students that, "Patience during the process, leads to faster progress." This applies to many life situations as well.

Awareness can wear many different hats. Let me give you some examples from the eyes of the golfing world. During a swing, when I see a student actually move or re-adjust their hands from the grip on the backswing, or at the top of their backswing, nine times out of ten when I bring it to their attention, they were unaware of this happening. Once it's mentioned though, they swing again, and it feels different during the motion, now it is a conscious thought their mind is aware of. This is the beginning of the change and a move towards better mechanical techniques.

Another example of mindfulness in golf, is when I take someone and do a complete evaluation of their game and begin to chart and monitor specific statistics from their play on the course, i.e. how many putts per round.

Once we have a starting point, and we find some weaknesses in their game and we can quantify them, the students become aware of how much of an impact it had on their score. They thought it was a weakness, but now they know exactly how much of one it truly was, simply because we were intentional about obtaining the information and gaining this knowledge. And as we all know, knowledge is power.

"Awareness is like the sun.
When is shines on things, they are transformed."
--Thich Nhat Hanh

With my own golf game, I had my learning moments and became aware of several things over the years. One that strikes me as the most important, would be when I became mindful of the fact that I was trying too hard to play good golf. I realized that there was a fine line between preparing properly and "trying" so hard to play well, that I was getting in my own way.

It wasn't that I didn't care, it was simply that I knew I had to stop pushing so hard to "make" something happen, instead of just simplifying and "letting" it happen. When I figured this out and changed my self-talk, my game took on a different meaning. I started playing golf much more relaxed and with a sense of gratitude, instead of self-induced pressure. When that moment happened, my acceptance of the way I approached my goals shifted from turmoil to grace.

I could say this was unfortunate, as I admit this happened in my later years as a competitive golfer, but that would be inappropriate, as it is *never* too late for awareness and improvement. It just happened later than I would have preferred, but I am thankful I had the good fortune over time, to be introduced to positive self-talk and neuroplasticity. This allowed me to experience the changes necessary for my progress and quality of life.

A quote that I often refer to regarding awareness and lessons in life, is from Robin Williams again when he says, "THERE IS A LESSON IN EVERYTHING, you will have bad times, but they will always wake you up to the stuff you weren't paying attention to."

Overall, my golf game and my life, were void of the 'missing link' of positive self-talk for a LONG time. Upon discovering this, and becoming more conscious of what was missing, everything changed for me. I began to see how all the links were connected and how, for all those years, the one link that might be *the* most important, had been missing…positive self-talk. Now it was time to connect them all!

I have referred several times to the book by Dr. Shad Helmstetter, ***"What To Say When You Talk To Your Self"*** for a very good reason. It is one of the best ever written and can change your life in the most profound of ways.

One of the exercises he has you do quite early in the book, is to go out and listen to how others are talking to themselves or what they are saying to themselves out-loud. Then, after doing that for a few days, he wants you to listen to what you were saying to yourself. Monitor your thoughts, your comments, your beliefs. What are they sounding like and how do they make you feel? How are they affecting your daily life?

Basically, with this exercise, he was wanting you to become more aware of self-talk in general, with yourself and others. This is how we come to terms with what needs to be changed and quantify our internal chatter. It is then and only then, that you can begin to monitor, edit, and replace the negative with positive self-talk to move towards your full potential.

I would like to make note of something at this point in time. I am referring to multiple words in this chapter that all have to do with awareness. Some of them include awareness itself, being self-aware, conscious, mindful, and recognition. I am making a point, in general terms, as each of them has its own definitions, but all are very much interconnected. Below is an explanation from Wikipedia that may help discern the difference between some of them.

Self-awareness is the capacity for introspection and the ability to recognize oneself as an individual separate from the environment and other individuals. It is not to be confused with consciousness in the sense of qualia. While **consciousness** is a term given to being aware of one's environment and body and lifestyle, self-awareness is the recognition of that awareness. The practice of Mindfulness involves being aware moment-to-moment, of one's subjective conscious experience from a first-person perspective.

"Awareness precedes choice and choice precedes results."
--Robin S. Sharma

About ten years ago, I learned of a concept quite interesting to me, called Baader-Meinhoff Phenomenon or another title for it is the Blue Car Syndrome (there are others, but we will stick to these two for now to make the point). Let's go with the Blue Car Syndrome, because this is personally how I became aware of it, as I was sharing my thoughts with someone and they brought this to my attention.

After hearing about it, I looked online for some sort of easy explanation and here is the best one I could find. It is succinct and exactly how I wanted to explain to you the idea of becoming more aware of things around you on a daily basis:

What? You don't know about Blue Car syndrome? It's like this: you've been fine with your old heap of a car until someone calls your attention to this new model of vehicle. It's blue and gorgeous, and you love it, but you're not really thinking about a new car right now, are you? Then, like magic, you see that blue car 10 times on the road in the next week. Where did they all come from? You'd never seen one before, and now, they're everywhere. Surely they didn't just all appear? No, of course, they've always been there; your brain just didn't identify them before.

Since that time, I have become aware of this approach to my thinking, and I can honestly tell you I have experienced this phenomenon many more times, pertaining to various things. I came to realize that if we live our lives on auto pilot, then our awareness level will not likely be challenged or changed.

We must pay attention to what is going on around us, so as to both engage in the happenings, and be able to make changes where necessary, so we can expand our horizons and live life more fully. This is exactly what happened to me with my trip to London.

It's empowering to understand that your own self-talk will either enhance an experience or turn it into a negative situation. Your life will then either be one of gratitude, grace, and acceptance…or it can be one filled with resentment, regrets, stress on a grand scale, and a belief that, "this is just the way it is." And let me tell you, **it doesn't have to be that way; you can re-create anytime you want…it is NEVER too late!**

Your paradigm of any situation certainly should have the key component of awareness, so as to give you the chance to make a decision on your self-talk. You make choices every day that determine the quality of your life, so why not start with how aware you are of your thoughts and choices, knowing you are in control of them, and begin to make positive ones, if needed.

I have been very candid about how Gratitude Golf, LLC came to fruition with the sudden, painful loss of my job in 2009. During the two years after I was dismissed, I remember when my husband would tell me that I was still angry and it would be helpful if I just talked about it, in an effort to try to calm down the storm in my soul. I would adamantly tell him I was not angry.

It wasn't until I became aware of my own anger, got in touch with my feelings, and began to realize I was still hanging onto it, that I could start to let it go, be at peace with the situation, and forgive those who had so terribly hurt me, in so many ways. At that moment, forgiveness became freedom.

It was also in that period of time, that I became conscious of the fact that moving forward, *no one* was going to dictate my future and decide if I was worthy enough to be working for them. I was just a commodity to those people, and my soul was worth more than whatever they were paying me to be their servant. I was determined to succeed and my self-talk became strong and confident.

It was in those painful but polishing moments, that I had to stop and reflect on what God's purpose was for me on my time here on earth. I needed to become aware of the path I was to take to give me the quality of life I was seeking and find clarity with what I wanted to do in my life.

Only when I stopped being so angry and started to find resolution to the conflict in my soul, that I was able to find peace. This took some very intentional positive self-talk, forgiveness, and conviction that everything was going to be alright.

"Awareness is Empowering."
--Rita Wilson

How aware are you of the path your life is taking right now, what is your journey like at this moment? How much awareness do you have when it comes to your golf game? Are you playing the way you want to play, or could it be improved with some intentional effort and gained knowledge? What is your self-talk like in both of these areas? Positive, affirming, being your own best friend, *or* negative, harsh, and being your own worst enemy?

To reiterate, your own personal awareness is very empowering, and if you start to bring it to the forefront, you will begin to embark upon a pathway leading you to the promise and potential you were born with. Somewhere along the line, you may have lost your passion for life and can't figure out what happened. The 'missing link' is a perfect place to start to regain that spark for life, to find once again, what makes your heart skip a beat.

Start to monitor your self-talk, become aware of your surroundings and watch what happens! If during the process, you stumble and fall, that's *okay*, just get up, shake the dust off, and start again. It's all part of the process. Being self-aware is not a guarantee against mistakes, but your ability to learn from them, and to improve, will make all the difference in the world.

One of the things I am so grateful for, being in the golf industry, is the fact that golf and life in general have so many parallels and lessons to teach us along the way. When you become mindful of what your self-talk consists of, and how it can affect your outcomes, you will be much more apt to increase the quality of both your life and your golf game. They will both be positively reinforced with a conscious effort to improve the quality of their essence.

I firmly believe that being a psychology and philosophy major, has made a big difference and been an asset in my abilities as a golf instructor and person dealing with everyday life. I am fascinated by the topic, and of course, intrigued when it came to the idea of awareness. This chapter is so important to me because I believe it speaks to the core values of who we are and what we want to do with our lives.

In general terms, an article on psychologytoday.com states that as humans, it is said we become self-aware sometime between 1-3 years of age. Some sources say we are born with a bit of self-awareness, but it really starts to take shape during the first few years.

What happens to it as time passes, will be shaped by our own perceptions and how we process our day-to-day experiences. I say this because it is important to recognize, who we see when we look into the mirror, as we get older.

During my schooling years while studying psychology and learning more specifically about the subject, I stumbled across something called the mirror test. From Wikipedia, it is described as, "Sometimes called the mark test or the mirror self-recognition test (MSR), is a behavioral technique developed in 1970 by psychologist Gordon Gallup Jr. to determine whether a non-human animal possesses the ability of self-recognition."

I have always owned pets and have fond memories of when our kittens or puppies first saw themselves in the mirror and thought they were playing with a friend. This display has provided me with countless memories of laughter and smiles. There is a myriad of videos posted online showing this epic cuteness.

Just as our animal friends are excited and playful when they see themselves in the mirror, so should we be! When we face ourselves in our reflection, wouldn't it be amazing to see unlimited promise and potential, just as it was when we were born? Wouldn't it be great to want to dance, be friends with, and talk to the person we see in the mirror?

How life-giving would that be, to feel so much positive energy from our own reflection, that we could do anything we put our minds to! It *is* possible, with the idea that we will forever be able to re-wire the brain in our thinking, and listening to positive self-talk. What a gift to ourselves, our family and friends, and the universe!

> *"Awareness is a key ingredient in success.*
> *If you lack it, seek it. If you have it, teach it."*
> *--Michael B. Kitson*

While writing this chapter, my husband Dean, walked past me and saw the mirror test portion and jokingly said, "Mirror, mirror on the wall, who is the fairest of them all? I said, "I don't know...who should it be?" His response to me was, "It should be whoever is looking in the mirror." I then asked him, "What if, whoever is looking in the mirror, doesn't like what they see?" His response… "Then that person should make some positive changes and then look again later."

When you look into the mirror though, just remember, **you are always enough.** Can you become a better version of yourself throughout your life? My answer has to be "yes," as I believe we can always learn and become more polished as we go along.

I am so grateful for the help from my husband, who is a retired pastor and was a counselor in many parishes, and how he has coached me over the years, training me to become an effective listener and coach. I can always get better, of course, but certainly it has been a very important tool for me on the lesson tee and in my personal life, to become an attentive listener and better person/coach.

Listening is one of the quintessential elements of awareness, as we must get in touch with our thoughts and how we treat ourselves in order to begin our journey. If you are discovering that you have been void of the missing link of positive self-talk in your life, now is the time to venture out on a new path of transformation. Because as we know…it is *never* too late to change!

If you listen to your self-talk and your thoughts, you can begin to monitor, edit, and replace with positive affirmations necessary for you to thrive. I have a picture in my house and read it quite frequently to remind me that I must continue to be conscious and attentive to the surroundings and happenings in my life, so as to be the best possible person I can be. It goes like this:

"Listening to your heart, finding out who you are, is not simple. It takes time for the chatter to quiet down. In the silence of "not doing" we begin to know what we feel. If we listen and hear what is being offered, then anything in life can be our guide. Listen."

GOLF LESSON FROM CHAPTER 7

We know that awareness is the key to change and challenging yourself while experiencing growth and improvement with your golf game. Discovery of the specific areas that need work is the first step and with the help of a trusted golf instructor, you will be able to identify more definitively, what your roadmap will consist of for practicing and playing. Develop a plan, stick with it and keep your thoughts positive. Make sure you talk to your golf instructor about your doubts and fears, they are real and you can eliminate them with the proper approach of applying the missing link. Elevate your thoughts to elevate your game!

LIFE LESSON FROM CHAPTER 7

With your own self-awareness, it is significant that you stop and take time to notice what is going on around you and what you as an individual, are experiencing. If you are not happy or comfortable with your life, make some changes. Evaluate what you would like to see change, write your goals down on paper, put a date on it when you would like to see them implemented and accomplished. If you are enjoying your life, then continue to be mindful of what is truly creating the joy. You can also share your insight with others to help them discover their path towards inner peace and acceptance.

PERSONAL REFLECTION AND INSIGHTS FROM CHAPTER 7

_____
_____
_____
_____
_____
_____
_____
_____
_____
_____
_____
_____
_____
_____
_____
_____

Chapter 8

HONOR

> "Life every man holds dear; but the dear man holds
> honor far more precious dear than life."
> --William Shakespeare

Reflecting on when I was first introduced to the word honor, a few situations come to mind. From more of a whimsical perspective, my earliest recollection of it was remembering it being said on my grade school playground with my friends. When one person challenged another, as to whether or not they were telling the truth about something, they would chant "I promise...Girl Scouts honor" while holding our fingers up in the air.

Now, upon saying that as a grade schooler and knowing that some kids probably wouldn't keep their word or tell the truth, for the most part, I really did trust my friends. I am sure I heard the word honor many times before this, but this is where it stuck out in my mind as one of the first times it applied to an actual life situation for me as a youngster. It was about honesty.

The next vivid memory of honor was when I learned about it in the Ten Commandments at church. It was introduced to me early in my faith journey as the fifth commandment of "Honor thy father and mother." If you could have experienced our family growing up in the 60's and 70's, you would know this was very much a way of life in our household.

Myself and three siblings, truly did honor our father and mother in every way. Of course, we had our disagreements now and again, as all families do, but at the end of the day, our parents were the rock, the ones we knew we could always count on. They were encouraging, supportive, and most of all, they loved us unconditionally. It gave us the opportunity to build confidence, learn how to respect others, and develop our own sense of self.

"It is a full time job, being honest one moment at a time, remembering to love, to honor, to respect. It is a practice, a discipline, worthy of every moment."
--Jasmine Guy

Our house was a safe place to make mistakes, learn about life, have fun, gather, invite friends over, laugh, cry, disagree, grieve, console, just about anything a typical family would encounter. So our gift back to our mother and father, was to honor them to the fullest…after all, through Gods work of the miracle of life, they gave us life!

As I have become older and experienced life a bit more, honor takes on different yet, deeper meanings. Today, when I think of honor relative to life, I think of integrity, friendship, and loyalty. Honoring our friends with loyalty, to the extent that we respect who they are and the gift they have become in our lives, is something we should certainly cherish and be grateful for.

Even just the simple honoring of another human being we may not know, because we are all connected, would make this world a better, more peaceful place to co-exist. Our communication with each other would be more positive and struggles would be minimized.

Years ago, I met a very special elderly woman by the name of Madeline, who passed away in 1997, but during the few short years we had together, we became good friends, and she, my spiritual mentor. She was a nurse from England, and also, served as a Sergeant in the Royal Air Force as an aircraft engine mechanic on fighter planes during World War II. When she would minister to the soldiers who were injured, she said they always talked about the endless blue skies in America, and from those conversations, it is the place she wanted to live out her life, and indeed she did.

She always had some words of wisdom to share with me and once said, "God, made everything and everyone different to have variety in the world; people, colors, animals, plants, food, everything you can think of! Imagine if all things were the same how boring it would be!" How true Madeline…how very true! These words Madeline shared, have helped me to honor the variety and specialness everyone brings into this world.

*"It is not our purpose to become each other;
it is to recognize each other, to learn to see
the other and honor them for who they are."
--Hermann Hess*

Some time ago, I was reading a book and came across the word NAMASTE. Since that time and with my personal understanding of the meaning behind the word, it has been such a blessing for me to look at others from this paradigm. It helps me to stay calm, understand everyone is different and know there is much diversity in the world, and that is okay.

Interpreted, it means "the Spirit within me recognizes and **honors** the Spirit within you." What a different place this world would be if we all approached life from this perspective.

Honoring one another would be a good start to restoring humanity's integrity and respect. An appropriate quote for this would be from Neville Chamberlain (1869-1940) in his speech after the Munich Agreement where he said, "I believe it is peace for our time...peace with honour."

So you might be wondering what this all has to do with golf? As you know, in golf, we interpret honor as something we offer our fellow golfers in a round when they have performed well on the previous hole. Upon reaching the next tee box, the golfer with the lowest score has "honors" and can tee off first.

This is to give them the respect and distinction of good play and makes them feel "noticed." The dictionary would state this type of honor as, "high respect, as for worth, merit or rank." This validation for a golfer can surely muster up some positive self-talk when you can take the tee box first, because of your good play. It is an accolade you want to hang onto during the round and try to keep the tee box for as long as you can.

I can tell you from experience it is very rewarding to hear someone say to you, "Go ahead, birdie golfer, you have the honors!" Once those words ring into your ears, your own internal dialogue is pumped up and ready to go--What a confidence builder!

On the golf course, observing "honors" from a distance is when you know someone you are watching in competition, gets to the tee box first, and you can assume they had the best score on the previous hole without actually knowing their score. I have heard parents say during a round, "Great, my daughter is teeing off first, that must mean she played well on the previous hole." This is always a reassuring feeling as a spectator/parent!

So let's now take a look at some viewpoints when it comes to honoring yourself as a person and/or golfer. The word honor also can take on a meaning of, "honesty, fairness or integrity in one's beliefs and actions." There is no better game, in my opinion, that teaches you honesty, fairness, and integrity to oneself and others, than the great game of golf.

"Without true freedom and some kind of honor,
I cannot live."
--Albert Camus

I see and hear people dishonoring these core values the game has to teach us, more often than I would like. I feel bad for them, as I believe they are missing the point, but hope someday they can begin to see what the game can teach them. Typically, negative self-talk is prevalent in this scenario, and this type of attitude leads to adverse conditions, affects your game and score.

And, on the contrary, a person honoring the game with these common core traits with positive self-talk, can find themselves on a path to greater things, such as character building and confidence. Let me share with you a perfect example of this.

One of my junior golfers drove off to college in the fall of 2015 and was playing in only her second collegiate tournament, and the college's first women's golf season ever. In the second round, she found herself in a situation where she hit the wrong ball. *No one* in her group or the spectators following, knew she hit the wrong ball...*but she did*. She called the penalty on herself, and at the end of the two rounds, was tied for first place to go to NAIA National tournament.

It was onto the playoff... and this young lady, who honored herself, her family, the game, and the college she represented, went out and won the playoff! Now that's what I call the epitome of honoring what this game has to teach you about golf and life. Being honest and having integrity in the moment, when one could have chosen another path, is what it's all about.

She chose the honorable path and was rewarded for her choice and the values she displayed. A quote from Sophocles will sum this story up perfectly, "I would prefer even to fail with honor, then to win by cheating."

At times, you will find yourself experiencing situations that may not be going your way. Honoring yourself as a person/golfer when this happens, is ultimately your true challenge. On the other hand, by verbally attacking yourself with constant criticism and never giving yourself and type of praise, you will only undermine your self-esteem and ultimately, your goals.

In addition to this, emotionalizing and personalizing the situation, with negative self-talk by saying something like you are stupid, an idiot for hitting it into that hazard, a terrible golfer, you always top it, you are a bad putter, you should have known better, etc. etc., you are only programming your mind to dishonor the authentic you. These actions will eventually break down the spirit within.

The key here is your awareness of the fact that the strongest program, or what we think most often in our minds, will win. Do you really want negativity to be the dominant program for your life? Do you enjoy being stressed out and feeling the effects of negativity with poor health, both mentally and physically? Do you want to play bad golf and dishonor the authentic potential in you, experience stressful times on the course, and rounds of golf filled with anger and frustration? I highly doubt it.

Always try to stay positive even when times are tough, to honor your character, your values, and stay connected with who you want to be out on the course, and in life, as well. This is a learned skill through repetitiously listening to positive self-talk statements. If at any time in your life, you do not honor yourself with compassion, you will then begin to jeopardize your full potential.

"Ability without honor is useless."
--Marcus Tullius Cicero

You were born with unlimited potential and perfect in God's eyes. Sometimes, in your journey, you may be exposed to elements that encourage or tempt you to dishonor yourself or others. It isn't anybody's fault, it just happens, but your awareness of how negativity can be damaging, is the beginning of turning it around.

It can be reversed. With a positive approach and self-talk, you can begin to acquaint yourself with the brighter side of your endeavors. With some very intentional effort to be more positive, you can create a new world for yourself. Go for it!

From a life perspective, one of the greatest displays of honor that I have been fortunate enough to see, is when the world stops to thank our military and veterans. With two of my children attending Ohio State University, and Nathan, my youngest son, being the 60th drum major for the marching band, I have seen some very emotional tributes of honor.

One in particular is when the alumni band puts on summer concerts for the surrounding communities. During the performances, they have a segment where they play all the various military songs, while asking the veterans to stand for public acknowledgement, thanking them for their service. To see them stand, salute, and sing their songs with such pride, is very emotional and truly an honor to watch.

Another incredible experience is when the Ohio State University Marching Band performs at the airport for the Honor Flights veterans as they come off the plane. To explain, an honor flight is conducted by non-profit organizations dedicated to transporting as many United States military veterans as possible to see the Washington DC memorials of the respective war(s) they fought, at no cost to the veterans.

"Honor to the soldier and sailor everywhere,
who bravely bears his country's cause. Honor, also, to
the citizen who cares for his brother in the field,
and serves, as best he can the same cause--honor to him,
only less than to him, who braves, for the common good,
the storms of heaven and the storms of battle."
--Abraham Lincoln

It is quite moving to watch these men and women get off the plane, be welcomed by a finely polished collegiate band, watch their family/friends greet them, celebrate their service with hugs and thank you's, and lastly, to see them cry with pride and joy for the acknowledgement from others. It is as patriotic as you can possibly get and something every American should see.

So, as I conclude this chapter, I would like to take one more look at honoring yourself, and will share with you one last perspective of honor. Honor is treating yourself with high respect or esteem. How much high respect or esteem do you have for yourself and for others? Would you like to make some changes that could put your life on a path to promise and potential? Have you reached a point in your life where you need to become your own best friend?

I am excited every single time a golfer stands before me on the lesson tee and wants to learn more about the game of golf. I see the promise and potential in all of you, and what is devastating, is what some of you do with your potential by rehearsing self-defeating beliefs and comments to yourself. This has no place in your life or your golf game, and is completely dishonoring the spirit within you. The 'missing link'—positive self-talk--can change all of that for you.

The obstacle or boulder you potentially place right in front of you during your learning process, is your own belief systems...they stop you dead in your tracks, and then you wonder why your game is not getting any better. This is precisely why I was originally going to title my book, "It's Much More Than Your Swing" because it truly is!

We both know it takes hard work to achieve the skills and improvements you are seeking. So, let's get you on track to an overall comprehensive game by including positive self-talk and honoring yourself. It's the best gift you can give to yourself.

This may be redundant, but I want to remind you that your instructor, whomever it is, can help you make your swing more consistent and upgrade your game overall, but in the end, if you internally continue to dishonor and disrespect yourself with negative dialogue and self-talk, it will impede your progress and your goals may not be reached...ever.

My wish for all golfers when you tee it up is, that you would honor the game, the people you are playing golf with, the beauty of the nature surrounding you, and of course, yourself. If you can be in the moment and mindful of how fortunate you are to be playing such a great game, things will remain in perspective and your enjoyment level will rise.

Honor...a word with few letters, but one that holds so much weight with its meaning, in so many various ways. Start today to honor yourself by recognizing the beauty and potential in YOU! It's unlimited and waiting for you to shine...go for it! NAMASTE!

GOLF LESSON FROM CHAPTER 8

Honor in golf is one of the finest character traits to possess. If you exhibit honor in the game, you preserve its historical origins and all that it has to offer you. Honor yourself and others you are playing with, to keep up the traditions. You owe it to the game, but more importantly, you owe it to yourself.

LIFE LESSON FROM CHAPTER 8

How much honor and respect you have for yourself will be an important contributing factor as to how happy you will be in your life. Keep honoring the spirit within you, and all the friends, family and acquaintances around you, and you will begin to see how much potential you have waiting for you in your life. The past is gone, the present is now, and the future is yours for the asking.

PERSONAL REFLECTION AND INSIGHTS FROM CHAPTER 8

_____

_____

_____

_____

_____

_____

_____

_____

_____

_____

_____

_____

_____

Chapter 9

PASSION

"Finding your passion isn't just about careers and money. It's about finding your authentic self. The one you've buried beneath other people's needs."
--Kristin Hannah

What exactly is it? Do you have it? Have you ever had it? If you don't, how do you find it? How do you know when you have found it? Some interesting questions to ponder about a word that has a plethora of interpretations. One of my favorite descriptions of passion I have read over the years is from Oprah Winfrey when she said, "Passion is energy. Feel the power that comes from focusing on what excites you."

During our lifetimes, and in different stages, we will feel passion in various ways, for whatever is facing us in our life at the moment. As a young person growing up, from about 3 to 10 years of age, I had a couple of things I felt very passionate about. One was music, and the other was to get out and play with my friends, play basketball, enjoy life as much as I could, just the plain old "being a kid."

I loved playing kick the can, dodge ball, cops and robbers...any game outside, and inside, I had my own little phonograph to play my records on and would listen endlessly to them, memorizing the words, singing my heart out! One in particular I remember knowing every word to was The Sound of Music. I loved Julie Andrews in that movie, and still do!

In junior high and high school, sports were it...all I could think about was becoming the best basketball player I could possibly be. Everything I did centered around the game, it was most definitely, my fondest passion! It gave me confidence and when I was playing it, I was on top of the world.

Of course, my parents made me focus on my studies as well, thank goodness, but basketball was my life in high school! I jokingly said I showed up for school because I wanted to make sure I was eligible for basketball, and of course, my favorite class was Physical Education.

Can you remember what your passion was in your younger years? Did it have to do with sports or something else that really made your heart skip a beat? It doesn't matter what it was, everyone has their own different areas where they love what they do. The most important thing is, we stop and ask ourselves some questions: When do I feel the most energy while in the midst of doing something? What makes my heart sing? When do I really know it's fulfilling my life's purpose?

As the years passed and life evolved, I found myself getting married at a very young age, and I believe my next real passion was raising my children, with my first husband, John. We truly were blessed with three of the most beautiful children one could ever ask for, and today, they are flourishing and making a difference in the world with their positive energy and inner beauty.

During our early years being married, and as far as John and I were concerned, golf was certainly at the top of our list as one of our passions. We traveled around the country to attend golf schools, took family vacations to play beautiful courses, were members at a local private club and began a junior golf program, to introduce young people to this great game, including our own children. As it turned out, golf would remain one of my truest passions throughout my entire lifetime because of those moments in the beginning of my golfing life.

The next phase of my life was after all my children were in school and I found myself wondering what my true purpose in life was to be. I began a very long journey of self-discovery at this point in my pilgrimage. I started to read many different kinds of self-help books, became closer to God in my faith life, and basically was searching for my inner passion.

"One of the many mistakes people make is that they try to force an interest on themselves. You don't choose your passions...your passions choose you."
--Jeff Benzos

Golf was always present in my life, but I didn't realize at the time, that it would take on a far deeper meaning and be a vehicle for me, with which I was able to hear the most important message for myself--to fill my own cup up first so I can help others, and also, to share an incredibly special message to the world...the message of positive self-talk and loving yourself

When I read Dr. Shad Helmstetter's book, **What To Say When You Talk To Your Self,** I realized that I wasn't "living the dash in my life". The dash between my first breath I took when my mother gave birth to me, and the last breath I will take whenever God calls me home. I want to spread the message of positivity to all of you who may be searching for something better, to those of you who are trying to find the meaning and purpose in your life.

It is definitely a process, but please know, it is essential you have positive self-talk to guide you along the way. It is the very tool and 'missing link' for you to begin opening up your heart and reconnecting with the potential you were born with. You must love yourself first for "being the incredible you" then you can focus on giving to others with love and compassion.

Are you in the middle of searching for a passion in your life? It sometimes takes a while to let the universe reveal what that is, but if you sit back and let things unfold as they will, life will expose to you the perfect reason you are here, with perfect timing.

Trust your intuition and let inner peace be your guide. Listen to your self-talk and what messages you hear to keep you moving in the right direction. Believe in yourself and the incredible potential and promise you were born with!

Every now and again, throughout my life, I have made choices that may have not been the best ones for me, but nonetheless, I made it. We all do that sometimes…make a decision when we likely knew wasn't in our best interests, but chose to anyway. This is the hardest part of life lessons.

Sometimes, though, we can even make decisions and honestly feel like they are the best ones in the moment, and with no regrets. It's definitely a learning process we go through from our choices and experiences, but it polishes our soul, and it is only then looking back in retrospect, we can accept that it was simply part of our journey.

Over the years, I wore many hats in the golf industry and had to make a *lot* of decisions about various things, and as I muddled through them year after year, I continually heard my calling to be the "teacher/coach" not the club manager or head golf professional. I was always drawn to the aspect of teaching golf and helping people, so I started to laser focus my energy on that area much more, and trust my intuition.

> *"Chase down your passion like it's the*
> *last bus of the night."*
> *--Terri Guillemets*

Every time I made a specific choice and found myself back in positions that did not involve teaching, I was truly an unhappy person inside. My inner voice was always talking to me, and once I began to listen to it more intentionally, I made a conscious decision to start my own company, Gratitude Golf, LLC. It was the best decision I have ever made, although it took some time to grow and learn how to run a small business, but it was worth every bit of effort I put into it...because it was my passion and I believed in its purpose!

So, as I continue to teach golf, with life moving on as it always does, I experience successes and setbacks, but through it all, I am always listening and learning, seeking out what my purpose on earth here continues to be, and living out my true passion in life. I am grateful for being in this position, and I am reminded every day, in many different ways, why I feel this gratitude.

A living example of this would be most recently in a comment on Facebook that my friend posted, portraying the darkness of life when you are not living out your passion. At work and feeling a gamut of emotions, she felt compelled to make the following post, "I wonder if anyone else's job can bring them through literally every emotion possible in one 8-hour day.... happy, sad, mad, glad, joy, failure, defeat, somewhat appreciated, un-appreciated, anger, relief, excited, alive, not alive..." My heart was heavy for her when I read this; I couldn't help but wish for her and everyone else, that they would be able to find their passion and live a fulfilling life they yearn for.

Confirmation from others is the best way you can be sure you have found your passion and are living it out. Often, while I am teaching and I express excitement about a student's achievement, with my own little celebration of a happy dance, they will stop and make a comment like, "You really love what you do, don't you, because it genuinely shows!" At first, it caught me off guard when they made this comment to me, but then I would stop and think about how many people in the world are truly doing what they love, and sadly, I realized... it's not many.

"Working hard for something we don't care about is called stress. Working hard for something we love is called passion."
--Simon Sinek

It is in that moment, I am filled with deep gratitude for this game called golf, for my beautiful students, and for the opportunity I have to be coaching them. I am so fortunate to be one of the lucky ones, living out my passion in my career. I saw a quote somewhere that said, "It's a beautiful thing when a career and a passion come together." Indeed, it is a beautiful thing, and I sincerely hope this will happen for you someday, if it hasn't already!

While in the midst of following your passion, there will be other opportunities appearing, that you could not even imagine. They are not planned, they are a gift from the universe, God, whomever you want to thank…and they are divine.

The road you are traveling on will have many stories and situations that lead you to where you are seeking to go, all the while, meeting messengers along the way. If you listen to positive self-talk, and you increase your awareness of the signs telling you which choices to make, your passion will come alive. Your positive self-talk and confidence will take you far in life.

This happened when I began my journey implementing positive self-talk into my life, and realized the importance and the impact it was making. As I mentioned before, I stumbled across the book *"What To Say When You Talk To Your Self"* and this is literally, when the inception of my new life started for me, both personally and professionally.

I began to share it with many people over the next few years, telling the story of how it had made such a difference in my life, and in doing so, I had high hopes it would enlighten their world too, just as it did mine.

To site a specific example of this serendipity, let me share a story with you. One day, years after reading the book, in my email inbox, I had an invitation from the Self-Talk Institute to become a Certified Self-Talk trainer and speaker.

My first thought was, 'Sure I'd love to do that, although I probably can't afford it,' but I looked into it anyway, just for kicks. With a bit of reluctance, I sent an email expressing my interest, and much to my surprise, a day or two later, I received a response asking for days and times I was available to visit with Dr. Helmstetter.

Again, I assumed it was all for naught, because surely this wasn't going to happen, as this was likely a form letter coming from somewhere in his office from the company, not coming from Dr. Helmstetter himself, he would never directly contact me! (Yes, that was very negative thinking on my part!)

And yet again, for some reason, I reluctantly, but curiously, responded, giving days and times I was available, and you guessed it…I received a response back, confirming one of the times! Now, I am really wondering what's happening and thinking this is too good to be true!

So, knowing the day and time he was to call, I said to my husband in the morning, "Guess what honey, I am supposed to get a call from Shad Helmstetter today between 9-11am EST. Sure...let's see if that really happens."

Lo and behold, in a matter of hours, I found myself visiting on the phone with the author of the book that literally changed my life, Dr. Shad Helmstetter, and shortly after that, I was chosen and invited by him to attend his certification seminar!

Upon meeting him at the seminar and in further conversation, he asked me to collaborate with him on a vision he has had for years, and he also inspired me to actually begin writing my book, after I had talked about writing a golf book for about 10 years or so. Since that life-changing day back in November 2014, he has become such a great mentor, friend, and inspiration to me!

Now, I find myself blessed with the opportunity to share with the world the message Dr. Shad has been researching and sharing for over 40 years, how important self-talk is, in every aspect of your life, including your golf game!

"Follow your passion, be prepared to work hard and sacrifice, and above all, don't let anyone limit your dreams."
--Donovan Bailers

None of this was an accident, it is a perfect example of synchronicity, and doing exactly what I was supposed to be doing by following my passion, by listening to the messages, the messengers, responding without really knowing what was going to happen, and trusting in what was to come.

I share this with you to highlight the fact, that all this happened because I chose to follow my passion, I listened to my heart, stayed on track with what I knew I loved to do the most, and from that point on, opportunities arose. You don't need to know what the opportunities are; you just need to believe they are coming your way. And as a bonus, the people I met along the way at my certification were some of the most amazing people in the world. These gifts called friends, when you make the right choices, will be the bow on the present in life, they color your world.

So on this journey, there is a bit of blind faith that must unfold when you are following your passion with signs along the way. When you think something is a "coincidence" maybe it wasn't a coincidence at all. In fact, it might be a great time to realize it's part of your destiny, part of the plan you are to be living out every day!

We all play such an important role in the quality of our lives, on and off the golf course. How you look at things and what you consistently believe to be true, will eventually become your reality.

I have spoken to my students for so many years, sharing with them the importance of positive self-talk and being your own best friend, in both areas of golf and life. I am 100% committed to increasing your awareness of this and connect the dots for you, so you know how truly important it is.

And even more so now, since I have met Dr. Helmstetter and found out about the scientific research studies and proof, that with the discovery of neuroplasticity, we can rewire our brains to help us reach more of our full potential we were born to experience. After hearing this information, and from that moment on…everything has changed with my teaching in golf and my outlook on life!

When I see students who really have a passion for golf, they can have different levels of goals for themselves, but in the end, their passion is what interconnects them, the commonality and bond is because of their love for the game. I have even heard someone say that when they come to the golf course every Tuesday morning, the other golfers there give her a sense of renewal in her life. So, in truth, you being YOU, is a gift to others, whether you know it or not.

I recall an older gentleman calling me up one day wanting to schedule his first lesson, and telling me a little bit about himself. One comment that struck me during the conversation, is when his voice got very animated and he said, "I know I'm older Alecia, but I just want to get better and have fun playing golf with my friends, because I just LOVE this game!" That, my friends, is passion.

"It is nevertheless a game of considerable passion…
either of the explosive type, or that which burns
inwardly and sears the soul."
--Bobby Jones

Whether you play for fun or take the game a bit more seriously, the overall experience you can own at the end of the day, will be either enhanced by positivity, or tainted with negative thoughts. You will ultimately make the choice, and whatever it is, you will then begin to program your thoughts in your brain, and your experiences and stories are the end result of what you thought and said to yourself. It's that simple, yet complex.

What superhighways are you creating in your brain? Are they the ones giving you the best chance for success? Or are they putting a damper on your results? So the stark reality is...you are the product of the programming you have been exposed to, whether directly or indirectly, AND you can change it at any time during your lifetime, thanks to neuroplasticity! What great news that is for all of us!

I see golfers passionately love this game, but at the same time, I also witness their self-talk as being so self-deprecating, they find themselves not enjoying it at all. You seek instruction, hoping to improve your game, and to possibly find the "secret"; you practice improperly (not intentionally) for hours, formulating unrealistic expectations, and then think you've failed miserably, only to find yourself still playing poorly. And, you may or may not have any instructor that talks to you about the mental aspects of the game and the importance of it.

Please understand, I am fully aware that a strong positive approach to your game, will not overcome a mechanical flaw. But because of negative self-talk while practicing and playing, the simple fact is, you will find every reason not to befriend yourself, (and maybe unknowingly), program yourself negatively. In another blunt way of putting it, you are living out self-sabotage. As I mentioned in another chapter, it is much more than your swing!

It's a slippery slope folks, and one you don't necessarily have to, or want to, get caught up in. I'd much rather you find yourself on solid ground with being positive and seeing how it can enhance your golfing experience, rather than inflicting your mind with negative self-talk. And remember, there are no failures here, only opportunities for learnings to happen in your life and on the course.

It is such a sad thing to watch someone get swallowed up by negative programming, as I know how much it affects your experiences and outcomes, **because I used to be that golfer.** I also know how much people love golf and want to play well and enjoy the moment, but often, they are not mindful of what the real problem is, and it's directly connected to their self-defeating thoughts and words, and not as much to their game itself.

My passion now is to help you all understand that a good portion of the "issues" you have with your game are not as much physical, as they are from your belief systems and programming, which a golfer would refer to as the "mental game" of golf. And, one needs to be practicing just as much on the mental game as they do on the physical.

And it's not only thinking positively and being proactive, although that is the first step, but it also must be combined with the 'missing link' of positive self-talk and rewiring your brain, and having this all-important combination, to maximize your experience. Couple this with working on your mechanics and you will increase your improvement percentages drastically!

One of the most diversified aspects of golf, is that it can be played by the very young and old, and everyone in between. Even the smallest of youngsters can have passion for it, as I have seen some kids who were only a couple years old and they constantly ask their mom and/or dad to take them to the driving range so they could hit some balls! My children were all introduced to golf at a very young age, due to our family's passion for it, and to this day, they can all go out and leisurely enjoy it, because they learned early in their lives, how to play and it was fun.

On the other end of the age spectrum, I have seen so many older people enjoy this game, such as my former father-in-law, Bud, who played as long as he possibly could. I believe he was in his 90's and still playing, because of his passion for the game he loved so much. He couldn't get enough of it. I even gave my former mother-in-law, Neva, a lesson in her early 80's, because she wanted to improve her game! Wow…I so loved the passion she had in her heart for golf and for life!

During my instruction in the winter months, I sometimes catch a glimpse of a gentleman who comes to the driving range, and I watch him hobble to a mat with his cane, replace it with his golf club, and proceed to hit a small bucket of balls almost every week…just because he LOVES this game. It's a beautiful thing to watch.

> *"There is no passion to be found playing small in settling for a life that is less than the one you are capable of living."*
> *--Nelson Mandela*

There are many stories from the young and old, and everyone in between, playing golf, because of what it has to offer us and the passion we all have for it in our hearts. It uniquely connects us, even without knowing one another, and what a gift to all of us from the game.

Inside the soul of the game of golf though, mesmerizing us while we stroll down the graceful fairways of heaven on earth, there is a lesson of another kind, waiting for us to find. It's real, authentic, different for everyone, and most of all, passionate about you and I discovering its beauty and grace. We can discover the lessons with friends, family, or all alone, it makes no difference.

What really matters is, that we ourselves, unveil the learnings and embrace them with dignity. It is then, and only then, that we can truly feel the games passion and the meaning it has in our lives, and we can't wait until we can push that tee into the ground on the first tee again, in our next round. It's all waiting for us...

GOLF LESSON FROM CHAPTER 9

Your passion for golf may have been immediate or took some time to develop. Either way, it's alive and in your heart, and what you will ultimately discover is, your experiences will be influenced by your thoughts. Follow your passion for improvement, enjoyment, and love of the game, and it will reward you in so many ways, yet unknown to you. Golf is the instrument with the passion you have for it, you are the notes on the page, and your experiences are the music being played out. As you are on the course, enfold yourself with peace and positive self-talk...and go out and listen to the beauty of the song you are playing!

LIFE LESSON FROM CHAPTER 9

You are moving at a very fast pace in life these days. My wish for you is that you are able to take a moment to be more mindful of the messages, the messengers, and coincidences in your life, that might very well be leading you to your passion. If you are already living in your passion, congratulations, that is truly what all of us strive for, at some point in our lives. May we all begin to open our eyes and hearts with compassion and love, to see and feel what is possible for us, all the while, helping us to reach our full potential with our individual passion.

PERSONAL REFLECTION AND INSIGHTS FROM CHAPTER 9

_____

_____

_____

_____

_____

_____

_____

_____

_____

_____

_____

_____

_____

_____

_____

_____

_____

_____

_____

_____

_____

_____

_____

_____

_____

Chapter 10

CHANGE

*"The secret to change is to focus all of your energy,
not on fighting the old, but on building the new."*
--Socrates

Being a psychology and philosophy major, this chapter probably is the most intriguing and has a certain degree of mystery to it, when it comes to golf instruction and life. It draws attention to the particular area of our lives where we might find ourselves in a love/hate relationship with…the idea of change.

The first liberty we have, is putting our life on a bit of what I would call "auto pilot" and this reveals how we humans are such creatures of habit. Happy with the way things are, with little intent to change, and, if and when change occurs, are highly agitated by patterns being disrupted, we can actually fear change.

Second, we may be high change agents and the idea doesn't bother us at all, in fact, these people actually long for it and seek to make it happen, change is invigorating to them. Lastly, we could be a combination of both.

I experience these three types of people abundantly on the lesson tee because the inherent nature of golf instruction is about change. I have those who are willing to change and take little time to adjust and adapt to the new feeling, I have those who, unfortunately, do not like change at all, and have a longer learning process, then those who tend toward the middle of the road.

I explain to them that the reason they are on the lesson tee is for me to make changes, and it might be in their best interests if they can to embrace it, sooner rather than later, for the betterment of their game.

One of the most common reactions to a change being made is people start talking to me or themselves out loud. I have heard many a student commenting on a feeling or shot during a golf lesson when I make an adjustment. They come up with the funniest words for change, but the most common one used is 'weird', oddly enough (pardon the pun!)

A lot of my students know this word has become one of my favorite responses while giving instruction. It indicates to me I'm on the right path to bridging the gap from old habit to new habit, and that the student is trying something new, something different. Michael Breed said is so succinctly in a workshop I attended recently when he said, "We take a student who feels his/her movements are 'natural', we make them feel 'unnatural' (which are the changes we are recommending), and then it begins to feel 'natural' once again after they practice it. Natural, to unnatural, and back to natural again. And the cycle repeats.

I am always quick affirm my student's efforts by saying "Great, thank you for saying that, because weird is my favorite word when it comes to instruction! It tells me you are open and willing to execute the changes I am suggesting, and I love to hear it…thank you!"

My intent is to put a positive spin on the change I am encouraging, and to let them know it's okay to feel "weird," and assure them that I am walking right with them through the changes, with positivity as our guide. Some additional words or phrases they use as an initial reaction are awkward, goofy, funny, not good, and I can't do that, to name a few, but weird is definitely the most common.

When asking people what they don't like about change, their response is, they are just not comfortable with it, even though change is exactly what they are seeking and expecting when they arrive at the lesson tee. It helps the cause when I inform them of the fact that they are paying for me to change something about their swing/game, and we chuckle because it is so true! I encourage them to be patient with the process, allow me to walk through it with them, and while doing so, they find it's not so bad after all.

Having the right attitude towards change can be a difference-maker. Case in point: in the PGA tournament one weekend, a golfer was experiencing pain with an injury and having difficulty swinging. In order to finish the tournament on the last day, he needed to make an adjustment in his swing, so as to not agitate the injury, and he actually finished the last day with a decent performance. What a perfect example of adapting and accepting change for the better, once you put your mind to it.

One day, my husband Dean and I were talking about change and I was telling him how people were struggling so much with it on the lesson tee. During the conversation, he said something I had never heard before and I said "Stop, what did you just say?" He repeated back to me, "You should tell your students to take the approach of 'change the swing (with whatever I am suggesting) and then swing the change', that might simplify it for them."

CHANGE THE SWING, THEN SWING THE CHANGE! A very nice play on words, but one that gets straight to the point. What a fascinating way to streamline the process and certainly one I will be referring back to it when teaching.

From a golfing perspective, there is change everywhere! We experience it with the weather elements, all the different types of clubs and lie of the golf ball, the different holes played and styles of courses, the different areas of the country with different grasses, and of course, the different people who we will play with, (whether we chose the other players or we were paired up with them).

"My putting strategy is simple; if you're not making putts, don't be afraid to change your technique."
--Louis Oosthuizen

No matter what, we will find ourselves having to deal with change and we must adjust to the elements, as the dynamics of the game or a round of golf, can be influenced by so many things. Remember the formula?

Potential – Interference = Performance

It applies here as well! Adjust to the change, less interference, better performance.

One of the first workshops I ever attended as an LPGA Golf Professional, was in Las Vegas and I had the experience of learning about how people perceive and process change. They were conveying a message to us through this exercise, that this is what we will be doing as golf professionals every day on the lesson tee with our students, and one of our greatest challenges we will face with our students... making changes.

During one of the sessions, we had to pair up with another attendee in the room, whom we did not know. We were to stand and face one another and stare at each other for approximately two minutes, visually recording in our minds, specific details about each other's appearance. Making note of things, such as what type of clothing we were wearing, any jewelry we had on, shoes, any kind of accessories, etc. etc.

After staring at each other for the two minutes, we had to turn our backs and make three physical changes to our appearance. Upon doing so, we turned back around and faced each other again, and then had to verbally tell the other what changes we could see they made.

We actually did this a total of four times, and the most intriguing part of this entire exercise, was during the last phase, people were trying to figure out what kind of additional changes they could continue to make, as all of the changes up to this point, were removing things. No one was putting things back on, which was an acceptable change in this exercise, because there were no set rules regarding this.

The point being revealed here was, the vast majority of people think that change is a negative thing, and they have to lose something instead of gaining something...when I change something, I lose. Looking at this from a golf instructor's perspective, I must be very sensitive and empathetic to this concept, as I am introducing change to my students on a regular basis.

Countless situations have reminded me how the smallest of changes can throw a student into a tailspin and the reactions I get from them because of an adjustment being made. It can be a pre-swing or in-swing change, neither one carries extra weight as being more negatively impactful to the process, in their minds.

One example of this, and the reaction very unexpected, is when I asked my student to make a subtle change such as the clubface being square at address and not closed. One students reply was "It is just too weird to look down there and be that much different, it messes up my whole swing!"

Now, we all know that it doesn't really mess things up that much, it's actually going to help them. But, to the student looking down and seeing the change, in that very moment from their viewpoint, it does make a *big* difference! Thus, it jeopardizes their swinging motion from the negative self-talk they were saying, which is then classified as interference, which in turn affects their desired outcome. Remember the formula?

This my friends, is *exactly* why golfers don't like change. At this very moment, you could argue "I did it better the old way" and you are not willing to see the big picture as to how the change is going to help you in the long run. Unless...I explain differently, and that is my job and obligation to you.

Most of the time, people are just verbally expressing their thoughts by blurting out their uncomfortableness with it, either directly or indirectly to me. I'm fully aware of the fact that the awkwardness will go away when they practice the change enough with repetition, and it becomes more "normal" to them, but the first initial reaction is unfavorable. Again, my job is to convey the message about the reasons *why* I am making the change, and then the transition will be more seamless, when it starts to make sense and you correctly practice the new habit instead.

Posture changes are another area for reactionary comments coming my way. When I suggest a change in your posture, for instance, you will have obliged to make the change during the lesson. But upon your return a week or two later, I see that your old posture may be right back in place. What this tells me is, you may not have practiced and done enough repetitions of the new posture, and your old posture was a stronger feel (program) and you defaulted back into it. And, as I have said at other chapters in the book, **your strongest program will always win.**

To some extent, I understand resistance to change, but it concerns me when it stops you from improving because you might be stubborn, or you don't practice the new habit with repetition. You quite possibly will never know your full potential if you don't change, because you are getting in your own way. You thus become an obstacle to yourself. All of this includes negative self-talk.

Similarly, in life, we can apply this to our self-talk, as we know scientifically, it is about repeating and listening to the positive audio statements. Without this, the old, stronger program wins and we will default back into our old life patterns. In golf, we can attach ourselves to the old habits in the swing and not change, telling ourselves "It's not going to work" or "I don't like it" and simply choosing to stick with the old habits, because they are seemingly more comfortable.

In either of those cases, there simply was not enough repetition to bridge the old habit into a new, more enhancing habit, which is a process we must repeat often to improve. We can also apply this concept to our self-talk on the golf course and our beliefs about what we can and cannot do.

> *"The only way to make sense of our change is to plunge into it, move with it, and join the dance."*
> *--Alan Watts*

If a golfer continues to believe that he/she gets nervous when facing hitting a ball over water, and they always hit into it, then technically, I could congratulate them for doing exactly what their mind thought about most, and it became reality! If we don't program ourselves to think positively in practice and on the course, and consciously improve and/or change our beliefs, then it can have a detrimental effect on our score and overall experience.

As I alluded to earlier, change can be somewhat of a mystery, and it bewilders me to know that students pay to receive golf instruction, knowing all along there likely will be changes made, and then grapple with them. Some older students will adamantly take the stand, that you can't teach an old dog new tricks. I'm not buying that one!

If that's what they say to me, they are really just projecting their own thoughts and programming, and telling me they're not willing to change. They have become entrenched in their old patterns, which is more comfortable for them and they may feel they are more in control.

Unfortunately, if you find yourself in this situation, your improvement may be slim to none, simply based on your belief that you may have rehearsed over and over, that you cannot change. This can make situations a reality for you and the danger is, it can lead to you not wanting to learn new habits. Truth is, you CAN learn new tricks, but you need to program your mind to believe in the idea.

Self-talk statements allow you the opportunity to re-wire your thinking and help you reach more of your goals. Being older does not make any difference. Age is not a factor when it comes to re-wiring your brain and making changes, thanks to the power of neuroplasticity!

On the contrary, I had a great conversation with a new student recently, and the comment I will share with you, was quite refreshing and rare. It was someone I had never met, and I was referred to him by his longtime friend and golfing buddy. He is 75 years old and very excited to arrive on the lesson tee as his daughter had purchased four lessons with me.

When we were finishing the conversation, he made the comment: "Okay, Alecia, I look forward to meeting you; I will bring my set of clubs with me, and also, a learning attitude. Thank you so much and see you on Wednesday!"

Wow!! What more could I ask for, than a student entering into a golf lesson with a learning attitude? What an incredible approach to adopt when facing change.

Here are some questions to ponder if you're a golfer. When your golf instructor made a change to something in your game, how did it make you feel? What did you say to yourself that maybe stopped you from making that change? Why did you possibly not want to make the change in the first place? Was it because you are stubborn, didn't understand, didn't like it, thought your old way worked better?

Or, if you did make the change, why were you obliged to do so? What are your beliefs when it comes to change in your game--do you like it or dislike it? Are you experiencing the 'missing link' on the golf course when it comes to your self-talk and belief about change? Have you ever thought that it might not be a mechanical change you need to make, but a different approach to your thinking while you are practicing and on the course when playing?

Bottom line is that life and golf are always going to require change, whether we like it or not. How we deal with this change will vary from person to person. Some are willing to accept the idea that changing elements are not always in their control, and then there are some who are not so willing.

These people are the ones who may be more frustrated with life and experience more stress. Personally, I think change, whether intended or not, brings about a sense of freshness and diversity in life, once you accept it and eventually muddle through it.

But I suppose one could debate this theory, by saying, a life without much change, is very comfortable and predictable. Both sides have their own argument, and it really depends on the situation we find ourselves in, as to whether or not change is necessary.

"All great changes are preceded by chaos."
--Deepak Chopra

I have had four major changes in my lifetime, in both my personal and professional life, and am so grateful for the fact that, in retrospect, I realize they have molded me into the person I am today.

All four were definitely life changing, very difficult to process, and certainly not planned, but I now realize the significance of the soul searching that occurred while I worked through them. The silver lining, I found in all four, made them a quintessential part of my spirit and my vision for life moving forward.

First, was my father passing away suddenly in 1995. One minute he was there, the next he was gone. My entire family, friends, and community went into shock with this loss. He was a very successful businessman, a giving and loving husband, father, grandfather, and the glue that held our family together. None of us were ever the same after his passing. The pain we felt was deep, penetrating, and suffocating. It took me at least two years to finally feel life again, but then, the next big life change happened.

In 1998, I found my marriage of 17 years ending in a divorce, and my world was once again turned upside down, along with many other people, including my husband's and the beautiful children we had together. It was heart-wrenching and difficult, being only a few years after my father's death.

Divorce is never an easy time in anyone's life and a difficult decision to make, for all the people involved, but I was facing it and needed to find a way to survive, for myself and my children. There was pain in everyone's heart and another life setback for me and our family, but I was determined to see myself through it and emerge a better, stronger person.

Looking back, I probably didn't realize how incredibly scared I was to start this new journey, but I was in the midst of it unfolding and had to find a way to cope.

I moved to Spring Green, WI for a Director of Instruction position, rented a home and dove right into my job. Alone, without my three children for the first time in my life, and for the rest of the summer, in a new community, a new full-time job with multiple responsibilities, and wounded, I desperately tried to embrace change with grace.

I found myself moving two more times in the next three years, because of my job, so I went from being in one town for 36 years, to moving three times in five years. That is the epitome of change, learning how to deal with it and finding a way to endure the chaos, while trying to stay balanced.

The third event was September 21st, 2001. I was giving one of my students a chipping lesson, when I was suddenly struck by a golf ball on my left temple. I was knocked out and when I woke up, all I remember is seeing beautiful blue skies with puffy white clouds passing by and wondering if this is what heaven really looks like.

When I heard the paramedics encourage me to take deep breaths of oxygen, as they placed the mask over my nose and mouth, I quickly realized I hadn't died, but the fear in my heart was immeasurable, as I thought about potential injuries and my children who were at school.

I was taken by ambulance to a local hospital twelve miles away, and remember the ER doctor telling me after he observed my injuries, that "I was one lucky lady to be alive!" He said another ¼" or so lower, and it would have been a direct hit to the temple and likely fatal. So while I was on medical leave, in October, the facility contacted me and said my position was going to be changed to seasonal, and without benefits.

I knew I must have a job year round, so I began searching on the LPGA website and found a year-round teaching opportunity at an indoor/outdoor driving range facility in Columbus, OH, and moved there in 2002. Yet another big change in our lives.

The fourth life changing moment happened in 2009, when, after I thought I had finally landed a great steady job at a private club as a Head Golf Professional, after two years of dedicated work for them, I suddenly found myself jobless.

It was a Monday, I was running an outing and had just put all the golfers out on the course. I was sitting at my desk, when I got called into the owner's office. The next few minutes were some of the longest in my entire lifetime, as I listened to them tell me they needed to prove to the investor's they were making "smart financial decisions" and because I was the highest paid employee, my position was now terminated.

As they spoke, I felt like someone was suffocating me, my heart was pounding out of my chest, and panic was the only thing I could feel. From my perspective, (and I found out later, from many others) I had no rational explanation for why they were letting me go. It wasn't fair or compassionate, but it was reality. The truth will never be revealed or heard, but that's okay. I know in my heart the reasons, and it had nothing to do with my work ethics or quality of my work, but all I knew was, it was another big change.

This was at 1pm and I was to be out of my office by 5pm. I was completely numb, as I packed my belongings in front of my oldest son, who was my assistant at the time, and other co-workers, and put them in my car, preparing to drive away from that place one last time. It was the most humiliating time of my life, both from a personal and professional prospective.

Once again, a major life changing moment. And for the next two years, I was truly a lost soul, as I later realized, my job had become my identity. I continued to give lessons, but did a very good job at hiding my emotional state of disarray. Angry, hurt, wounded, hopeless, despondent...you name it...I felt it. My self-worth and self-esteem just hit an all-time low. I didn't have the missing link.

After a year of being angry and unsure, I took a $9.00/hour job working in a cubicle selling small gifts and crafts over the phone. I also bounced around and took jobs at a well-known chain DIY stores and within three months was offered the manager position at the customer service desk, and lastly, an hourly employee at a national pet store chain.

The pet store job was the final straw for me. Every day I found myself in a glass enclosed "play room" full of different-sized dogs, mopping up their #1 jobs, shoveling up their #2 jobs, and logging them on a clipboard! I found no pleasure in continuing this type of job for any amount of time. I became conscious of the fact that I deserved so much more than this from life, and I had to make a change or this was heading in very much the wrong direction! I almost lost my house, my golf students, my social life and friends, my second marriage, and my desire to live.

Then suddenly, after wallowing in my pity and letting despair hold me ransom for two years, I realized, **if I want something to change…I must change.** I re-assessed my goals, forgave myself for what I considered failures in life going all the way back to high school, (they really weren't failures, they were learnings), and made a conscious choice to change, for the better.

Not having many resources, and still wounded, the only thing I knew to do was what my mother taught me at a very young age. She said, "Alecia, doing kind deeds for other people will always make you feel better about yourself." So I did just that, I took action and began to do kind things for other people.

In December of 2011, I decided to make changes in my attitude, goal setting, vision moving forward, and basically how I was going to start to live life, instead of feeling like I was dying while my heart was still beating. I knew that God had a plan for me and I was going to start listening to the messages and have faith in the journey.

So it was, that I started moving forward with ideas I had on starting my own company. After a very long conversation with Dr. Kathryn Sullivan, the first woman to walk in space, and also student of mine, I met with successful businesswomen she connected me with in the Columbus area.

I was seeking feedback from them about my ideas, feeling very vulnerable, but dared to be great, as Brene' Brown would say! It was in those moments, that Gratitude Golf, LLC was born and my life has been forever changed. The premise of my company was to give back in every possible way I could, and express gratitude with all my endeavors, personal and professional.

With very few resources, I started giving back to people one step at a time, and it worked! The actions I took created a feeling of benevolence and my heart started beating again for life! I was alive and for a change, I actually started to feel it!

Looking change straight in the eye, acknowledging and being okay with all of the various feelings I was experiencing, I forged ahead. I knew I could do it, and knowing what my vision and purpose was, gave me momentum and a new start on life. I look back now, and am thankful I lost my job as a Head Golf Professional at the private club. I feel I am the lucky one to get out of such a toxic environment, even though in the two years of pain and despair, it certainly didn't feel like an opportunity.

The gifts that have been bestowed upon me, with my new company, and after the job loss, far exceed anything I could ever have done sitting behind a desk at a club. What I learned is that one must have the will to keep pressing on and believe in themselves and in their calling, then with time, the change will become fruitful and positive.

In all four life situations, I encountered change in the most intense way, the kind that hit you in the core of your heart and soul. But people can grow from those moments, you just have to get through the fire, symbolically you become polished, like an agate. You find out how strong you can be in the deepest moments of pain, during this refinement process called "change."

Change in our daily routine, albeit more mundane examples, can also put a wrench in our rhythms and patterns that we have established over time. It can easily throw us off in the moment. Ultimately, it's our self-talk, and how we process the variation, that can take us on a road to new possibilities, or it can keep us on the same path we've been traveling on, with a less than desirable outcome and added stress.

We need to be mindful of what we say to ourselves in these situations that can either help or hinder our process of dealing with change. This is a critical factor when changes are happening: being mindful of what our self-talk is like in the moment.

"Change brings opportunity."
--Nido Qubein

What are you saying out loud or in your mind, that has you dealing with the elements of change? What are your beliefs about change? Have you dealt with it well in the past or not? Were you calm or did you let your amygdala fire up and take over your rationale? It might be time to take an inventory of sorts, make some adjustments, if necessary, and you may find yourself on your way to new patterns and potential and accepting change!

This is important for me to pay attention to when teaching, as it affects how willing and committed my student is to making the changes I am suggesting. They may understand while they are with me in the moment, but the more important question is, how will they be while practicing on their own? Will they have positive self-talk when faced with adversity during the changes?

If your self-talk is not positive and strong, and you don't know precisely what to practice with intention, you will likely set foot onto a platform that is filled with doubt and fear, and revert back to old patterns. You could then start to believe that golf instruction isn't worth it, and we know that's not true. Moving forward, golf instruction really needs to have more emphasis put on the importance of the 'missing link' combined with the mechanics, and the realization of how that potent combination can change everything!

I recently had a young junior golfer talk to me about her game and the lesson was not so much a mechanical golf lesson, as it was a mental game assessment. After much conversation, we discovered that she knew exactly how to be self-sufficient when it came to making minor swing changes relative to her game and tendencies during her practice sessions and decision-making on the course.

She did it consistently on the lesson tee with me, but through our conversation, she began to realize she didn't trust herself while out playing competitively, to make those same changes and decisions on her own. Because of her lack of trust with the change, she jeopardized her fundamentals and chose to make compensating errors to try to hit the ball straight and play better, which only produced more errant shots and her misses were more consequential.

"In the game of golf, the degree of adjustment to a repeatable swing is only within a few degrees. In life, it is very much the same. Tiny changes lead to huge results."
--Unknown

From my experience in both golf and in life, I have seen change precipitate more fear than it does hope, for a better outcome. We all desire a positive outcome, we have good intent, but we get so stuck in a rut with our negative thinking and our attachment to the outcome, we can't seem to find our way out.

The process of changing something, gives us the desired outcome we are seeking. So the willingness to accept the necessary change, believe in your heart and mind the goal is achievable, makes the expectation much more realistic.

Positive self-talk on both accounts will have an incredible influence on one's ability to change and acceptance to move forward, even though it may feel uncomfortable in the moment.

I want to add that I have been referring to change in a deep, profound, sense of the word, but it doesn't always have to be that kind. A more whimsical look at change could be something as simple as buying a new car, moving to a new home, reading a new book, taking up a new hobby for a change of pace, painting a room in your house a new color, or choosing a new hair style. All of these are examples of what fun change can be!

The life lesson I have heard many times over, about how one needs to feel uncomfortable in order to experience growth, is profound relative to change and how we process it in our minds and in our life.

How do you look at change? Are you scared of it? Is it a positive or a negative force in your life? Are you willing to change so that you can finally start to reach your full potential? Are *you* ready for a change?

I'll finish this chapter with an incredibly inspirational piece about change. A couple years ago, I was researching this topic on the internet, and I ran across the following article, written by an engineer. I didn't write down the specifics of author, when it was written, etc. and my apologies to them, but I was so enamored with it, I had to keep it in my file. It is absolutely *the* best way I could ever try to explain what change represents.

I make copies and give to my students on the lesson tee regularly, so they have a perfect summary of the ebb and flow of change and what it can be for all of us in our journey called life. It is so succinct and profound, that every time I read it, I appreciate change all the more.

I hope that if you are one wrestling with change, this may help to re-align your thoughts about it and open up a new world with unlimited potential. May you enjoy it as much as I do! It's titled *"What is Change?"*

Change is something that presses us out of our comfort zone. It is destiny-filtered, heart grown, faith built. Change is inequitable; not a respecter of persons. Change is for the better or for the worse, depending on where you view it. Change has an adjustment period which varies on the individual. It is uncomfortable, for changing from one state to the next upsets our control over outcomes.

Change has a ripping effect on those who won't let go. Flex is the key. Even a roller coaster ride can be fun if you know when to lean and create new balance within the change. Change is needed when all the props and practices of the past no longer work. Change is not comforted by the statement 'just hang in there' but with the statement 'you can make it'. We don't grow in retreat, but through endurance. Change isn't fixed by crying, worrying, or mental tread-milling. Change is won by victors not victims; and that choice is ours.

Change is awkward—at first. Change is a muscle that develops to abundantly enjoy the dynamics of the life set before us. Change calls our strength beyond anyone of us. Change pushes you to do your personal best. Change draws out those poised for a new way. Change isn't for chickens.

Change does have casualties of those defeated. Change will cause us to churn or to learn. Change changes the speed of time. Time is slow for the reluctant, and yet it is a whirlwind for those who embrace it. Change is more fun to do than to be done to. Change seeks a better place at the end and is complete when you realize you are different.

Change is measured by its impact on all who are connected to it. Change is charged when you are dissatisfied with where you are. Change doesn't look for a resting-place; just the next launching point. Change is only a waste to those who don't learn from it. Change happens in the heart before it is proclaimed by our works.

Change chaps those moving slower than the change itself. If you can change before you have to change, there will be less pain. Change can flow or jerk, depending on our resistance to it. Change uses the power invested in the unseen to reinvent what is seen. Change is like driving in a fog—you can't see very far, but you can make the whole trip that way.

Change is here to stay...

GOLF LESSON FROM CHAPTER 10

Change in your golf game is a constant, as we are always challenged to improve through our development as a player, both in our mechanics and the mental game. The natural elements change daily as well, as Mother Nature always has her part to play in what we deal with. Our challenge is to embrace change, feel it's presence, and realize, in the big picture, it's all part of the process and we will forever have to adjust.

LIFE LESSON FROM CHAPTER 10

Your life has a natural ebb and flow of change built into it. From the moment you were born, your life has been changing. Ride the waves of change, know that it happens, and look for the good in all of it. Keep in mind that when you feel uncomfortable while change is happening, you may feel a little vulnerable. It's part of the growth process and you will feel more confident when time passes...*it's okay!*

PERSONAL REFLECTION AND INSIGHTS FROM CHAPTER 10

Chapter 11

TIMING

"Timing is everything. If it is meant to be, it will be. Everything happens at the right time for the right reasons."
--Maya Mendoza

According to one definition, from the Free Dictionary, *timing* is the regulation of occurrence, pace, or coordination to achieve a desired effect, as in music, the theater, or athletics. This applies well to a golf setting.

For life in general, what we think of as *good* timing, is related to *synchronicity*. That is, things working together in what seems like a happy coincidence. *Bad* timing, in this sense, would be the opposite—everything working out in the worst possible order or arrangement.

It is with absolute perfect timing, that I sit down and start to write this chapter! Seriously…perfect timing. The older I get, the more I tell myself that timing is everything, and the events that take place are unfolding just as they should and when they are supposed to.

Now, I know you could probably debate with me at some level on this one, but if you really stop to think about it, you have likely encountered many "coincidences" in your life. There could be a chance that your awareness was such, that you maybe didn't realize the impeccable timing as to when they happened, but it was still ongoing, noticed or not.

Yes, there are some things that happen to us and we can honestly say, "What bad timing that was," but I would guess there are just as many times we could say, "Wow, what perfect timing!" I rely heavily on my own awareness and personal self-talk to notice my timing experiences. This takes intention, awareness, and repetition to rewire one's brain, but it can be accomplished. It's merely a new habit you can implement.

Here's a personal case of serendipitous timing I can share with you from my past. I recall a moment in my life while I was living in Spring Green, WI and was home for the afternoon, as I took a sick day from work. I was very sad and had been crying for what seemed hours. This was my first summer without my children after my divorce, and the first time I had ever lived anywhere but my hometown. I was all alone in my home that certainly didn't feel like a "home" yet, and my heart, well, it was very broken.

In my first marriage, I wasn't able to have a cat because of allergies in the family, so when I got divorced, it was one of the first things I wanted to do, rescue a cat. I went to the shelter, found the perfect match for me, and upon going through the adoption information, I found out I needed my landlord's permission before I could adopt her. My landlord denied my request, and I was devastated, back to square one, and my heart was still heavy.

Later on that day, when a new friend I had just met recently, rang the doorbell, I tried desperately not to show my pain and disappointment, but I was certain she felt my heart hurting. The house was dark, all the shades pulled down and it was the middle of the afternoon. She saw the red, puffy eyes from crying and in an instant, we both knew there was a reason she was standing there at my front door.

She claimed she stopped by just to say "Hi," and check in on me. But I couldn't help but wonder…why right then? Why at a moment when the world felt like it was coming down hard on me, and I felt very vulnerable and alone? How did she know I was at a low point? Whatever the reason, I later knew it was perfect timing, and she told me later that she felt an "impulse" to stop by the house.

Was it a higher power speaking to her heart and sending her a message? Was her intuition so strong she knew it was the right moment? Was it me sending out energy into the world that I was hurting? You can choose to believe any or all of those thoughts, but what I do know is that this type of thing happens to me a lot.

> *"There is a time for everything, and a season*
> *for every activity under the heavens."*
> *--Ecclesiastes 3:1*

I am fully aware of the timing of the universe and how we are all delicately interconnected. Because of my personal self-talk, these gifts occur more often along the way. I am filled with gratitude for the "coincidences" that occur; I know that my self-talk influences them, and I stop to give thanks for them.

As I get older, this idea of timing becomes even more relevant and I have an acceptance level about things happening in my life, that is much greater than before. I have begun to acknowledge that when situations unfold, they were on the timeline precisely where they were supposed to be.

This idea, at times, can be challenging, as we human beings sometimes want things to happen on our time and when we want it, not when the universes timing brings it on. It may occur much earlier or later than we anticipated, and we may not fully understand it in the moment. Frustration can set in quickly, if we are not careful.

An example of this, would be my earlier story of me losing my job. I thought it was the worst timing in the world, but if I would have had more positive self-talk at the time (the missing link), the adjustment period from the entire situation, would have been a much easier ride. This is when I strongly believe the 'missing link' of positive self-talk can help you see from "the bright side" instead of from a negative viewpoint.

Often I have been in a conversation with someone who says they are praying for God to hear their voice when they want/need something, and God doesn't seem to hear them or answer their prayers. I, myself, have also sat in a church pew, been on my knees in the quietness of my own home, or maybe while I am in a silent place reflecting, intentionally praying for some sort of help or comfort from a higher power. I don't know when the answer will come, but if I am in tune with the spirit of timing, I have a much greater chance of noticing the grace when it is bestowed upon me.

Sometimes, this grace can come not from prayer or thought, but happen in an instant, during daily life. It might make you stop, take a deep breath, and be grateful everything turned out fine. It might be the moment when you can literally say to yourself, "I am lucky to be alive!"

This recently happened to me when I was going to drop some important papers off at an office in downtown Columbus. On my way there, I stopped at a drug store for some items I had been wanting to pick up for some time. After making the purchase, getting into my car and driving to the stoplight, I realized I was going to be late, but for some reason, I said to myself that I would get there in time and there was no need to rush.

Slowly creeping to the light to make a left-hand turn on the green arrow, I had this sensation come over me to hesitate. Just as I was deciding to move forward, I looked up and in a split second, saw a car coming *very fast* from my left, running the red light, and missing me by a few feet. The other drivers sitting in the intersection were showing signs of shock in their faces, as I am certain they figured I was going to be t-boned by this guy and gone in an instant.

Luckily for me, I was spared the disaster of a serious car accident, or possibly death. In that very moment though, I realized that if I had been in any kind of hurry, my life could very well have been over. I have had several of these types of situations happen to me recently, and it truly makes a person stop and appreciate that we must live one day at a time.

The timing of my hesitation, the guy speeding through the red light, angels watching over me, and the fact that I could drive away from this situation with only a scary memory, is what I would call perfect timing filled with grace.

Now let's take a look at timing from a golf swing perspective. I often have told students that timing is the toughest thing I teach, because it is so abstract and ambiguous, and due to the fact that it is the golfer who is in charge of the motion, not me. I share this even though I know they understand what good timing is, but making it happen when you are swinging anywhere between 50-100+ miles per hour, is somewhat difficult to execute and master.

> *"Rhythm and timing are the two things which we all must have, yet no one knows how to teach either."*
> *--Bobby Jones*

I have lovingly titled timing the "Holy Grail of Golf." Everybody wants it, seeking endlessly for it, but not sure how to capture it...it's elusive. Timing in a swing, or the sequence when the mechanics are supposed to happen, will potentially be one of the biggest challenges you attempt. There are certain elements of your swing that should happen in the right place at the right time for high efficiency impact to take place.

The problem? We human beings/golfers often interrupt the motion in the timing with our impulses of reactivity and anticipation of the "hit" or impact. One of the definitions I have for the golf swing is uninterrupted motion, and when you can achieve this, then you are focusing on swinging the club, and not hitting the ball. This will give you a much greater chance of carrying out better timing, with a positive outcome.

If you swing in the proper sequence, then contact with the ball will be incidental, and is, for the most part, a luxury. That is if you swing and not *try* to hit the ball! You see, we call it a golf *swing* for a very profound reason; we are seeking that particular motion.

You don't want to perform a golf chop, a golf hack, or golf lunge, do you? When you interrupt the motion in the swinging process, you probably will feel the movement being uncomfortable and hard work, rather than having an effortless golf *swing*.

"Timing...the most difficult, abstract concept I teach,
yet one of the most important elements to achieve."
--Alecia Larsen

A critical component to this is what you are thinking **before** and **during** your motion. I frequently share with my students that I refer to the incidental contact as the "Oops Rule." You swing from top of your backswing to follow through and **oops**... the ball got in your way. This is what happens when you focus on the *swing*, and not the *hit*. It's a whimsical way to say, swing on a specific path and the ball will disappear.

It is very unlikely that you will ever hear me say 'nice hit' to someone on the golf course or on the lesson tee. I like to encourage you with the statement of 'nice swing' instead of planting the seed in your mind to hit the ball. Even though I am fully aware of the fact that this is what the game of golf is all about--hitting and advancing the golf ball around the course--a hitting mentality creates a jerking motion, flinching, and a swing that looks like it is in many disjointed parts, instead of a swing with flowing motion. Therein lies the definition of uninterrupted motion.

The cycle begins at address, with your self-talk, when you start with the thought that you must "hit" the ball, rather than swing the club, and most certainly your motion will be jeopardized. It sets off a ripple effect of inaccurate timing, and this, my friends, is the kiss of death in your golf game. If you address the golf ball with the paradigm and self-talk that you will swing the club, your chances of a decent outcome increase dramatically.

I don't know of any sport that doesn't require efficient timing of some sort. On the lesson tee, I often refer to when a quarterback drops back to throw a football. Once the ball is snapped, he looks downfield to his receiver and he is going to have to execute the pass with precise timing and accuracy, so as to lead his teammate, anywhere from 15-50+ yards away, for a reception.

Moving parts, emotions, human error, weather, defenders, and other additional elements, will make this task challenging, but with precise timing, many catches are made each and every game. Same goes for many other sports; timing just happens to be one of the common threads in all of them. If, for whatever reason, it is off kilter, the chances of you executing a good shot will be reduced, just as reception of the ball in football may not be complete.

*"Every person fulfills their purpose
when the time is right."
--Unknown*

This is true, and even more so, in competition, when there is something on the line and you may have more adrenaline to deal with. Excess adrenaline, anxiety, negative self-talk, doubt/fear, are just a few of the feelings that can alter your timing drastically.

I remember listening to Payne Stewart up in the press box at a major PGA tournament after his play one day. He said that all golfers will be challenged with the concept of maintaining the timing in their swing, especially under pressure. It is human instinct to want to "hit" it!

When teaching, it is imperative that I talk about timing and when things should happen during motion, but my main job is to help you stay focused on one thing at a time, to keep things simple and clear. If you attempt to execute multiple things simultaneously while trying to master one specific skill, the odds are that you will become confused and frustrated quickly. This will alter your self-talk and send you down the path of having thoughts filled with hesitation and uncertainty. The skills you are trying to learn will then become more difficult to acquire, instead of becoming new habits that lead to better shots.

Having a tool like self-talk for golfers while you are developing your game, both in practicing and playing, will enhance your learning process and help the timing of your swing develop more efficiently. This undoubtedly will promote confidence and enjoyment. As a side note, instructors should try and stay away from giving students too much to think about, as this will, most definitely, affect the student's outcome. Our minds cannot process multiple things at once, especially while moving at a very fast rate of speed.

The timing of instruction as to when you get the parts to make the whole, is paramount to how you will build your golf swing, whether you are a beginner or have played golf for any amount of time. Again, if you try to do too many things at once, the mind will always default to what has been repeated the most, or the one thing your mind focuses on in the moment. It could be your new habit or your old one, depending on which you have given the most focus.

I remember early in my career, having the unique opportunity to meet a sports psychologist by the name of Chuck Hogan. He told me that helping students stay focused on one thing, is essential to their progress. When I moved to Columbus in 2002, I reached out to him and was searching for some insight regarding half hour lessons, as I had not given many of them up to this point; they usually were an hour long.

My question to him was, "Can I really get the message across to my students in only half an hour? This would mean that I can only really talk about one or two things at a time." And his answer was one I will never forget! He said, "Ahhh...Alecia, be careful, sometimes in a lesson, two thoughts can be one too many!"

WOW! The idea that we should not overload our brain while practicing, is something that I believe golfers tend to overlook. It is *so* tempting to keep "trying this or trying that" to make sense of the swing, but it really only complicates things when you do too much at one time. It seems golfers love to think about a million things and attempt to become the jack of all trades and master of none, and this too, has a direct influence on timing.

For this reason alone, you must realize the sequence of *when* things happen in your swing, to be able to recognize what needs your attention first, then build on that, focusing on one issue at a time, to complete the process. For example, I feel that all golfers need to have strong, sound fundamentals before we can move on to some of the more advanced mechanics of the swing.

Focus on what you intend to change, and then give it all your attention. This will give you the greatest chance to succeed, keep your mind clear, and promote positive self-talk during all the developmental stages.

To summarize my thoughts in this chapter about timing and regarding our daily life, I believe the events that are happening around us constantly, are on our timeline precisely where they are supposed to be. Situations take place, in our daily life and in our golf game, where timing is of the essence. Moments occur with grace, seemingly without any of our efforts to help them transpire. These moments that unfold are effortless, enlightening, and always welcome. We sometimes call them synchronicity or "being in the zone."

> *"Life teaches us to make good use of our time,*
> *while time teaches us the value of life."*
> *--Unknown*

Remember those times when someone very special entered into your life, as if by chance? You may have been in need of their presence, as a resource to something bigger and better, or an angel in the form of a friend, was sent to you, to help you deal with hard times, or just simply someone you know who called you at the perfect time, when you needed it the most. What did you say to yourself when that moment happened? Were you grateful for it or did you write it off as a coincidence?

How about with golf...remember the time you hit a golf shot that was so exceptionally good and you have no idea how it happened? Or the hole where you got your first birdie? Why was it so easy to execute? Chances are you just relaxed, you were swinging the club with rhythm, your timing was efficient, and your outcome was positive. This breeds confidence and positive self-talk, which produces even more good shots.

In either situation, in life or golf, enjoy those moments when timing is impeccable, and accept the fact that sometimes, when timing is not so good, it's just part of the process. None-the-less, timing is an important part of our lives and very much a part of golf. What is certain, is that each of us must learn to deal with both the desired and less-desirable outcomes. It is the 'missing link'--the self-talk tool—that will help us deal with it, and can change situations from the mundane to miraculous.

GOLF LESSON FROM CHAPTER 11

When it comes to timing, with your golf swing, there may not be another equally-vital element for regaining your rhythm, when you really need it the most. It is a matter of controlling your internal compass, staying calm and trusting, to allow the physical experience to take place smoothly, in the few seconds it takes to perform the swing, putter through driver. Know the sensations, feel the balance and be aware of the sequence that will give you the outcome you desire.

LIFE LESSON FROM CHAPTER 11

Timing is a vital element in life in general. Sometimes it works for us with perfect precision, and at other times it can go wrong in a way that seems not so kind. What we all must be aware of, is the fact that we can be the person who follows their intuition at just the right moment to help another in need, or at other times we can be the recipient of the perfectly-timed assistance from another. Either way, timing is an interwoven thread of what we call "our life." Listen, hear, and watch for the signs, and chances are, you will be surprised at what will unfold. Grace abounds!

PERSONAL REFLECTION AND INSIGHTS FROM CHAPTER 11

Chapter 12

PERSEVERANCE

"With ordinary talent and extraordinary perseverance,
all things are attainable."
--Thomas Foxwell Buxton

In choosing the chapter titles for this book, I knew that this one on perseverance would carry substantial weight in the big picture of both golf and general life.

In addition to the meaning of its impact in our lives, the deep connection that self-talk and perseverance have with one another, is indisputable. When dealing with difficult times and when we feel like giving up, is when the quality of our self-talk counts the most. This will be the tipping point when we choose to either keep moving one foot ahead of the other or stop in our tracks, depending on our what we choose.

The actual definition of perseverance is; "To persist in anything undertaken, maintain a purpose in spite of difficulty, obstacles or discouragement; continue steadfastly." This definition alone, motivates me to keep going, and helps me see the true meaning behind the word.

My own journey with obstacles in both my life and my golf game, has had its ups and downs, to say the least. I am grateful for those moments when my heart was singing with joy, but I know all the while that this emotion wouldn't have been as strong, had I not gone through some hard times prior to that. It is likened to the yin and yang concept where one aspect of life cannot exist without the other.

From the Ancient History Encyclopedia online, I found a succinct way to describe this concept that confirms why we will not go through this life without encountering both, as it has been around for centuries.

Yin and Yang is a fundamental concept in Chinese philosophy and culture in general, dating from the third century BCE or even earlier. This principle, is that all things exist as inseparable and contradictory opposites, for example female-male, dark-light and old-young. In this philosophy, yin and yang (also, yin-yang or yin yang) describes how opposite or contrary forces are actually complementary, interconnected, and interdependent in the natural world, and how they give rise to each other as they interrelate to one another.

I am certain that all of you could sit back and reflect on how your life experience has been filled with the yin/yang theory, and how through those times, it has polished your skills with perseverance. I know that I have had my fair share, and that my self-talk either propelled me forward or held me back, in every situation I faced.

I must say though, back before I had ever read Dr. Shad Helmstetter's book "**What To Say When You Talk To Your Self**," my awareness level of how much my self-talk influenced my outcomes, was pretty low. It was only when I read the book that awareness got to a level where I understood its impact, and that it made such a big difference in my overall outlook on life.

When I began to look back, connect the dots, and truly realize that my self-talk was the steering wheel of my life, I was able to re-direct my thoughts to a more positive outlook. It was at this time, that I could begin to take charge of my life, set new goals, and have a vision that I could set my sights on, instead of being down on life and feeling sorry for myself.

One of those times, certainly had to be when I knew it was a make or break moment in my career. I had to decide if I wanted to stay in the golfing industry, and if so, what I wanted to achieve. My own self-esteem was very low, but I listened to the voice in my head saying that I needed to begin to pay it forward, give back to the world, somehow…some way.

With a determination that being depressed and feeling blue all the time was simply *not* going to defeat me, I sat down by myself at the end of the year 2011, and made some new goals. With a bit of blind faith and consistently reading positive self-talk banners from Dr. Shad in my email inbox every day, I pressed forward. Within months, I started to feel different. My paradigm was changing; I felt energized and refreshed. I had changed my self-talk and it was working!

From a family perspective, I recall some difficult times being a single parent, working a full-time job, and feeling that I wasn't going to be able to handle the pressure and responsibilities combined. I worried that I wasn't being the parent I wanted to be, but knew, that in order to provide for my children and basically survive, I had to work hard. This took a great deal of energy and time away from the home.

*"Patience and perseverance have a magical effect before which
difficulties disappear and obstacles vanish."
--John Quincy Adams*

My kids were an integral part of our coping with this, as they understood our situation and always seemed to help me through it, in their own special way. Specifically, I remember my sweet daughter Erin, in her young innocence, but wise beyond her years, standing at the edge of my bed one night saying, "Don't worry Mom, it will all turn out alright, God does not give you any more than you could handle." That always seemed to comfort me in times of trouble. Perseverance was my active choice and one of many gifts from my daughter.

When have you found yourself dealing with a situation that you just didn't think you could handle? How was your self-talk during those moments? Did it lead you down the path to making positive choices or down the path to outcomes you may not have preferred? Understand that you, yourself, have the power to make the choice when faced with these challenges, and the choice will determine the level of your perseverance **and** your potential outcomes. It gives you the internal insight to go one way or the other, and without it, your ship will sail aimlessly, with no specific direction.

In my personal life, I can honestly say that one of my strongest pillars of reminding me to "hang on" is a bible verse I ran across when my father passed away. It has been a rock for me ever since, during times when I felt like the world around me was closing in and becoming dark…it became my light to a brighter outlook. It is from Romans 5: 3-5, *"We all rejoice in our sufferings, because we know that suffering produces perseverance; perseverance character; and character, hope."*

Sufferings, for each of us, can take on a different meaning, but yet they can all fall under the same universal umbrella, when it comes to how we feel. They are not fun, may break our hearts, and challenge the deepest part of our soul. But knowing that suffering produce perseverance, gives me hope.

Our coping mechanisms will differ as well. I happen to rely on the scripture verse to keep things in perspective for me. What are some things you use to keep you from giving up? Is it music, positive sayings, scripture, poetry, walking in the garden, singing? Whatever it is, hang onto it, because it will be what keeps one foot stepping ahead of the next, for movement to continue.

"If you can't fly, then run, if you can't run, then walk, if you can't walk, then crawl. But whatever you do... you have to keep moving forward."
--Martin Luther King, Jr.

Finding strength in those moments with positive self-talk, both speaking aloud and in the thoughts you choose, can help you develop this trait. Your character becomes stronger and you gain confidence, and then you begin to have hope for a brighter tomorrow. It's a ripple effect on your day, months, years, and life that can have a significant influence on the quality of your existence.

Reflecting on perseverance in golf, I believe it could possibly be one of *the* most important qualities a golfer can possess. Golf is a game that can challenge and tax your patience very quickly, and if you don't have the necessary mental toughness to persevere, you will not likely achieve your goals. If you *do* make the conscious effort to develop mental toughness, you will have a greater chance to achieve them.

Having perseverance as a golfer, is not necessarily a visible trait, however. It takes on a quiet form of determination that people often find difficult to describe. You may see it when someone stays focused on their goals even in times of great challenge, they keep practicing, no matter what. They understand the entire picture of what makes their golf game complete. I liken it to having a strong 'heart' and 'desire' to achieve, even when knocked down a time or two.

You may see it when someone makes a triple bogey on a hole and then turns around and makes a par or birdie on the next hole. This could also be classified as resilience, which is very similar to having the trait of perseverance. The key factor in having the ability to rebound from a challenge on the golf course is positive self-talk, or the missing link. ***It is the force behind the action.***

On the flip side, a downward spiral on the course can lead to exponentially high scores and blow-ups that a golfer can regret after the round is over. I have heard hundreds of times, if not thousands, a golfer admitting they played alright for 14 or 15 holes, but had blow-up holes that cost them the great round they are seeking and they gave up, either mentally or physically.

What caused the meltdown? What was the learning in the moment, that could help you the next time it happens while you are playing in the middle of a round? How can you learn to intercept the negative emotions and redirect, so it can be a more stable round? By implementing the 'missing link' into your daily routines--*that's* how you can do it! It's simple, and effective, and it produces *results*, *if* you stick with it. It's about repetition.

I realize there could be an interesting debate here about good shots and making you feel more confident about your game. And, on the contrary, you could say that bad shots will produce negative thinking. But if you really understand the 'missing link', then you will understand that by rewiring your brain and programming yourself in advance of the golf course and while practicing, you will have a coping mechanism to deal with those shots that are less than desirable. Yes, they are inevitable. But the new habit creates the ability to cope.

Practicing this mental aspect of your game with as much intensity as your practice your mechanical or physical side of the game, will definitely produce a more positive experience overall.

Think of it this way. You are on the course, you hit a bad shot, your self-talk turns negative, you beat yourself up, and then you approach your ball to hit the next shot. Are you mentally ready for it *or* are you still seething about the last outcome?

"Perseverance is stubbornness with a purpose."
--Josh Shipp

Now, think about this scenario. You are on the golf course, you hit a bad shot, your self-talk is positive and you begin to reframe your thoughts to prepare for the next shot. You are more relaxed and playing in the present, instead of the past. Are you mentally ready for it? Is your mind clear so you can focus on the next shot at hand? Remember, the most important shot in golf is the next one...

Perseverance is powerfully affected by the quality of your self-talk, or lack of it. It's in the moments of emotional turmoil one needs a coping mechanism, to stop yourself from falling into an emotional abyss on the golf course. *This is one of the key factors to a golfer's ability to deal with stress, they need the "mental armor" of the missing link, to combat the negativity.*

During a playing lesson a few years back, I had four well- established junior golfers out on the course and I was observing their play. Strolling down the fairway, I asked one of the players what they would like most to get out of this playing lesson. Her response, "I would really like to know how to get a handle on my emotions after I hit a bad shot, or have a bad hole. How do I cope with that and turn things around, so it doesn't get real ugly?" What a great answer, and something I believe millions of golfers around the world would like to know how to do!

So when you are on the course, one could ponder as to what came first...the bad shot, then the bad attitude, or the bad attitude, then the bad shot. Did your poor self-talk lead to an undesirable outcome *or* did your undesirable outcome lead to poor self-talk? Clearly, one directly effects the other, it is a cause and effect situation. And, with each and every golfer, it will fall solely on your shoulders as to how it will affect your attitude and score. It's somewhat of a controversy, but as a golf instructor, I would highly encourage you to always listen to and practice positive self-talk, because in the end, that is what will have the biggest impact in your game.

As we all know, the opposite of perseverance is giving up. Giving up mentally in the middle of a round is *not* an option, if you want to score well. Giving up on your goals in golf is *not* an option, if you want to continue to improve. I love to remind my students that, "When you feel like quitting; think about why you started." Why did you start to play golf? What motivated you to want to play one of the greatest games in the world? When you feel like giving up mentally or physically, be strong and have positive self-talk...don't quit!

"Perseverance is failing 19 times and succeeding the 20th!"
--Julie Andrews

My golfing experience with perseverance came mostly with my hard work ethics on the mechanical swing itself, I worked *extremely* hard to make my swing repetitive. Unfortunately, I did not couple that with working on my mental game, so there was an imbalance in my game. I recall occasions where I never gave up and had mini-successes, but mostly, I remember being too hard on myself mentally, and this became a deciding factor in my outcomes. It is something I regret, to this day, and I will always wonder "what could have been."

Perseverance is something that springs forth from the mindset you carry, so if your thoughts are predominantly negative, then you are not likely to bear this important character trait. However, because you can continuously rewire your brain until you take your last breath, you can now begin to manage your thoughts and strive to include perseverance in your game, and in your daily life.

I have witnessed a good number of species exhibit perseverance, but when it comes to the squirrel, I am not sure too many can top them. They have such a tenacious quality about them that sends a message of never giving up, it is quite incredible. Stop sometime and watch them bury a nut, it is fascinating. There is something about the method to their furiousness, that is intriguing.

A while back, I read an article about business and using a squirrel's behavior as a metaphor and thought I would share it with you. Written by Associations Now magazine and the article was titled, "Squirrel Sense." The author, Francie Dalton, mentions five different qualities of a squirrel that exhibits with their behavior that we can learn from:

1. They are willing to turn themselves upside down to get what they want.

2. They are able to ignore their wounds and keep going.

3. They are willing to be treated as pests if it helps them succeed.

4. They are able to accomplish amazing feats because they're willing to try what others believe is impossible.

5. They are unconquerably persistent (as evidenced by those singularly ineffective "squirrel-proof" bird feeders).

Ms. Dalton mentions that overcoming challenges requires relatively quick access to your inner reservoir of resourcefulness, (which is what I would call your self-talk).

So let's take a look at those five traits from both the golf and life perspective and ask ourselves some questions. First, let's go with your golf game. Questions to reflect on would be something like the following:

a. Have you been willing to go the extra mile and practice all the components of your game properly to get what you want out of it?

b. Are you able to look past your previous disappointments and defeats on the course, turn them into learnings, and press forward toward the goals for your game?

c. Are you ready to take on the challenge of someone else ridiculing you for your efforts or for liking golf, in general? Do you compare yourself to others and try to be like everyone else, so as to not stand out in the crowd?

d. Do you have enough belief in yourself, and in your dreams for a better golf game, to not let anything stop you from achieving them, because you believe nothing is impossible?

e. Are you willing to be persistent with your work ethics in practicing all the areas that make up your score, with repetition, in an effort to achieve success?

Now, let's take a look at some questions that might apply to your life, relative to how the squirrel exhibits perseverance.

a. We all want and/or need things in our life, and there are times when we really need something extra to make it work. It may take that added effort on your end to make it happen. Are you ready and willing to do that?

b. Have you been hurt by someone or something in the past that is stopping you from moving forward, to experience a fresh new start?

c. Do you have the confidence to ask others for help with something, to obtain different points of view, so you can look at all angles?

d. Can you look at situations with confidence that anything is possible, if you put your mind to it?

e. If faced with a specific task, can you go to any length to get it accomplished, so that, in the end, you can say "I did that!" and know you conquered and succeeded in whatever you set your mind to?

By considering your answers to each of these questions, I believe you will be able to identify where some work needs to be done, in the area of your own perseverance.

> *"Great works are performed, not by strength,*
> *but by perseverance."*
> *--Samuel Johnson*

Back in 2011, when I wrote my goals down on paper, they became more real and tangible. I encourage you do the same. Then you can quantify what needs your attention, make changes, and improve. Put dates on them, list any obstacles, and then come up with action plans.

In my certification for becoming a positive self-talk trainer and speaker, Dr. Shad Helmstetter shared with us a great metaphor for perseverance. He told us that we are all on a journey and a road to success, with whatever goals we set. Make sure that everything you do on that path, the choices you make, the actions you take…are ones that will serve you to reach your ultimate goal. Keep moving forward with those things that serve you, step away and move on, from those that don't.

In my time on golf courses, I have seen so many squirrels scurrying around, looking for and hiding nuts, digging frantically for whatever reason. No matter what their intent is, it is with great purpose and they have a goal. Watching them, I get the feeling that behind their actions, is a mindset of never quitting, continually moving with ease, determination and perseverance, curiosity, playfulness and frolicking, nurturing one another, companionship, preparing to store their food for the winter, and overall enjoyment of the task at hand.

When I think of golf and our life as we know it, and I look at all those traits, I can't help but wonder... if we all took that approach to how we live, wouldn't life be a lot more fun? Take a look at all of those descriptive words again...never quitting, determination, perseverance, preparing, curiosity, playfulness, enjoyment, nurturing, companionship. Are there any of them that you wouldn't desire to attain and apply to your golf game or life?

There are many other species that we could study and say there is a correlation between what they do and what we should do as humans. But the bottom line is, we are of the species that can actively and logically choose our path in life. Most other creatures are just incredibly authentic; they act on instinct and they don't know any other way to operate.

So, find that place in your heart that is open to all there is for us to experience in life. With less stress, more enjoyment and gratitude, and an overall acceptance for what comes your way. Life will deal you the yin and yang of it all, but how you deal with it will be a deciding factor in your quality of life. It is your level of perseverance that will get you places you have only imagined.

> *"Perseverance is the hard work you do after you get*
> *tired of doing the hard work you already did."*
> *--Newt Gingrich*

In closing, have you ever flown on a plane and during the ascent and take off, you witnessed rising above dark clouds and rain, and you emerged into a beautiful blue sky for as far as you could see, with the sun brightly shining? I've always loved this moment, and felt this was symbolic for persevering in life.

There will be dark clouds, gloomy and gray days, rain, etc. But if you believe, that just on the other side of them, just above you and not far away, the sun is shining and waiting for you... you can prevail. You can persevere, dealing with all of life's ups and downs with grace, if you just believe in yourself and the potential for a positive outcome. *Nothing is impossible with the missing link of positive self-talk...*

GOLF LESSON FROM CHAPTER 12

On the golf course, there will be times when it will feel like the "golfing gods" are not on your side and luck is not in your favor. It is then that you must make a conscious choice in your mind with positive self-talk, to override the negativity by taking control of your emotions and reframing your experience. You must be in control of your emotions, don't let your emotions control you. Facing adversity with a positive frame of mind, is the start of implementing perseverance into your game. Never give up on a hole, a round, or on yourself. Your potential is unlimited.

LIFE LESSON FROM CHAPTER 12

There have been many times when I felt like I just wanted to throw in the towel and give up on things happening around me. But when you stop and think about it, perseverance is a great coping mechanism to help you through those hills and valleys. On a day that has more than its usual gloomy moments, I stop and tell myself that "this too shall pass." This is very effective self-talk for personal growth and getting through the day. And, lo and behold, it does pass, tomorrow is a new day, and there are still many people who love you for who you are. You ARE enough!

Hang on to the conviction that everything is going to be okay, you are going to make it! I have a very dear friend who I frequently will remind, in conversation, "It's all good!" And you know what? It truly is, find the glass half full and see the good in what's happening! Persevere and you will be more content and apt to experience satisfaction and gratitude in your life.

PERSONAL REFLECTION AND INSIGHTS FROM CHAPTER 12

_____
_____
_____
_____
_____
_____
_____
_____
_____
_____
_____
_____
_____
_____
_____
_____
_____
_____
_____
_____
_____
_____
_____
_____
_____

CONCLUSION

When I first read **"What To Say When You Talk To Your Self"** *by* Dr. Shad Helmstetter, I remember literally weeping at one point in a chapter. It was when he was bringing to our attention the fact that you were alone when you take your first breath, and you will be alone when you take your last. So don't allow anyone else but *you,* to define what the dash is, in between those two breaths.

You are the artist who paints a new picture each and every day of your life, as to what it will look like, and how it will feel when you step back and take a look at it. As far as I am concerned, self-talk is the single most important element in our lives that we have control over, when we say something to our soul, and how we treat ourselves.

Yes, I realize that others can say something negative to you, and it will be recorded, but you must be vigilant to bypass the negativity and replace it with words that describe yourself and your life *exactly as you want it to be.* Your awareness of this key point, is critical to monitoring negative input and replacing it with the kind of information that works in your favor. I saw a motivational banner a while back and it said, "Love yourself first, because that is who you will be spending the rest of your life with."

When I do presentations or bring up the idea of self-talk, I hear a lot of people say, "For sure, I talk to myself all the time." And they say it with a bit of jest in their voice, as if it is something that is being mocked or made fun of. Self-talk can be fun, but on the other hand, it can be one of the most potent poisons you could possibly ingest, and negative self-talk will make you slowly wonder why your life is so difficult.

To this point, I was giving a presentation to about 90 middle school students last year, and when I asked the kids what they learned from today's gathering, a young girl raised her hand and said, "Well, my friends and I have sometimes said things to each other, that weren't so nice, but we meant it as just kidding. Now, I realize we were actually harming one another by programming each other with negative self-talk." How powerful is that?

When I began to realize this personally, (both in my life and in my golf game), I then began to become keenly aware of what my students were doing to themselves with their own self-talk and how they were creating their own obstacles. I suddenly began to take this much more seriously. It took on a life of its own, and one with a message so powerful, that I simply could not ignore it any longer.

I had to share, not only the message with all of my students and others, but now I can share the fact that there is a tool, the 'missing link' that *you* have access to, available at your fingertips, to help improve your golf game and your life. It is revolutionary and you are the lucky beneficiary. Now *that's* exciting!!

I have put a great deal of thought into some key points that I want to make sure you keep in mind as you conclude reading this book. These are specific thoughts I have covered in the chapters, but are very important and worth reiterating to you. They are in no particular order of importance, but each of them is *very* important.

First, I want my readers to know that when it comes to your golf game, **it is *so* much more than your swing!** Golfers come to me every day, wanting to improve their game, and that is all fine and dandy. But, if during that process, they self-destruct and use negative self-talk to sabotage themselves, then they will not make as much progress as they'd like, and continue to think they are failing. Let me say this to students in this situation: You are *not* failing, you are just not combining the right self-talk with the mechanics, to make a potent, *winning* combination.

Golfers who have worked hard on their games or even those who are just learning, need the key component of positive self-talk to reach their full potential and enjoy the process. You may be one of those golfers who spends hundreds, and maybe even thousands of dollars on golf instruction, but if you do not have the 'missing link' component, it will be a rougher road to travel, and one that still may leave you wondering, "what could have been and what is missing."

Next, I want to bring to your attention something I feel is overlooked by most, and that is, your golf game consists of other important factors, in addition to the mechanics and mental toughness of your swing.

When I talk to my students about their game, especially my new students, I will show them a picture on the back of my business card that shares a point I want to make. That is, there is a delicate balance with what makes up your golf game, and I have seen it time and time again, when golfers may not know how important all these areas are to their overall experience.

Typically, then, he/she continues to believe it is their swing that is the problem, when in fact, there is little to no attention paid to the other areas, such as the mental side to golf, equipment, their commitment level, and their physical condition and strength. Even when golfers hear that "golf is 90% mental," they still don't give it enough love.

Keep in mind, I completely understand that no strong mental game, will ever compensate for a mechanical flaw or a lack of solid fundamentals, but what I am saying is, you need to have all the components to really make the machine work. If I chose the two components people tend to focus on the most though, it would have to be the mechanics and the mental aspect of golf.

The main purpose of this book is to raise your awareness of the fact that you need to work on the mental side of the game, **as much as** or **more** than you do the physical portion of golf. The two need each other, and you need them both, so you can enjoy the game at a higher level.

Let me ask you a question. If you knew two people, and one was very successful while the other was not as successful and fell under the less than average category, which one would you likely want to emulate? Which one of those two people would you like to walk with on the same path and rub elbows with? For purposes of making my point, let's put this story into a golfer's perspective, and call the person who is very successful, Player A, and the other person, Player B.

Now, Player A is committed to practicing diligently, they have an instructor they trust, they love golf, play as much as they can, are competitive, content in their personal life, and a good 'student' of the game, that is, they seek knowledge about it, work hard at it, and when they play, keep their emotions in control. They have a very good demeanor while practicing and playing, and generally speaking, they seem to have a good demeanor in life. They listen to positive self-talk consistently three times a day, and their scores for 18 holes range anywhere from 78-86.

Now, Player B is committed to practicing diligently, they have an instructor they trust, they love golf, play as much as they can, are competitive, content in their personal life, and a good 'student' of the game, that is, they seek knowledge about it, work hard at it, and when they play, keep their emotions somewhat in control. They have a very good demeanor while practicing and playing, and generally speaking, they seem to have a good demeanor in life. They **do not** listen to positive self-talk consistently three times a day, and their scores for 18 holes range anywhere from 83-91.

Yes, Player A and Player B sound a *lot* alike don't they? Except for one thing…listening to self-talk. I know that I just quantified, to some degree, the number of strokes it could potentially cut off your score, but having been in this industry a long time and teaching for almost 30 years, I can tell you that a 6-shot difference is a reasonable number to estimate, when talking about a golfer at this level, who listens to self-talk and then one who does not.

There are 18 holes to play, and when you think about it, 6 shots are one of a few scenarios; 3 double bogeys, 2 triple bogeys, 6 bogeys…well you get the point. If you look back and evaluate your round, most of your higher scores will typically come after you lose your cool and cannot maintain positive self-talk in the moment. Even though you probably know you talk to yourself, you likely talk to yourself *way* more than you think. And, if you monitor what is being said, you may find you are being very hard on yourself. This is where the scores start to soar upwards. Remember earlier in the book when I told you I wanted to title this book, "It's Much More Than Your Swing?" Well, that is precisely because *it truly is much more than your swing!* You are throwing away many shots during a round of golf because of the negative self-talk going on.

This suggests questions for you, once again. If you were going to bet on a Player A or Player B, which one would you likely choose? If you knew that listening to self-talk would enhance your game by 6 shots, would you be willing to take the time to listen to it? Are you willing to add self-talk into your schedule that would only take 30-45 minutes a day? Would it be that difficult to listen to self-talk while you were practicing your golf game? You could also listen to it in the car on the way to the course. What a great time to do that! If listening to self-talk enhanced not only your golf game, but your personal life, wouldn't it be worth your time?

What I do know from the experiences on the lesson tee, is that I have literally seen the power of positivity make an incredible difference in my student's outcome. Literally, when they proclaim what they want, it is with certainty that their outcome will either be what they desired, or much better than what they might have had if they had not set their mind on staying positive. Making an "I AM" statement is powerful beyond your imagination and if you say, "I am going to hit this shot right at the target, chances are you will!

The Missing Link is all about what is in store for you should you make the choice of implementing positive self-talk into your life. It is an exciting time, because 1.) It has been scientifically proven that your brain can be re-wired to think more positively; 2.) You now have the tool at your fingertips, and 3.) It's waiting for **YOU**!

Self-talk is here to stay, in fact, it has been around for centuries, we just haven't paid as much attention to it as we should have, and we were not aware of how much it can affect our outcomes, until recently. You are largely in control of your outcomes and the quality of life you experience. Positive self-talk is intriguing, influential, foundational and so empowering that you will find yourself wanting more of it, once you start listening to it. What's your choice? Which player do you want to be like? What kind of difference do you want to make in the world?

Today is a new day, tomorrow will be one as well. I encourage you to make a choice today, that will make a difference in your tomorrow. I leave you with this quote to ponder on, as you begin to reflect on your decision to make a conscious choice implementing the missing link of listening to positive self-talk statements, into your golf game and life...

**"A YEAR FROM NOW, YOU MAY
WISH YOU HAD STARTED TODAY!"**

"Love yourself first, because that's who you'll be spending the rest of your life with."

To order your positive
self-talk programs, visit
www.gratitudegolf.com,
click on 'Services' and then
choose 'Self-Talk Products' to get
started TODAY!!! ☺

If you would like Alecia Larsen to
speak to your organization, athletic
team, corporation, or business, send
an email to:
alecia@gratitudegolf.com